Camera Obscura

Camera Obscura
Of Ideology

SARAH KOFMAN

Translated by Will Straw

CORNELL UNIVERSITY PRESS
Ithaca, New York

First published in France 1973
© Editions Galilée 1973 *Camera Obscura*
English translation © 1998 The Athlone Press

Publisher's note.
The publishers wish to record their thanks to the
French Ministry of Culture for a grant towards
the cost of translation.

First published 1999 by Cornell University Press

Library of Congress Cataloging-in-Publication Data
Kofman, Sarah.
   [Camera obscura, de l'idéologie.   English]
   Camera obscura : of ideology / Sarah Kofman : translated by
Will Straw.
      p.   cm.
   Includes index.
   ISBN 0–8014–3641–9 (cloth : alk paper).—ISBN
0–8014–8593–2 (pbk. : alk. paper)
   1. Ideology—History.   I. Title
B823.3.K613   1998
140—dc21   98–39015
                                                       CIP

ISBN: 0-8014-3641-9 cloth
0-8014-8593-2 paper

Printed in Great Britain.

To Alexandre
To Jacques Derrida

Contents

Translator's Acknowledgements

In 1993, the magazine *Public* asked me to translate a portion of this book for inclusion in their seventh issue. I am grateful to Christine Davis, Janine Marchessault and, in particular, the late Sarah Kofman for their assistance with that translation. In completing this translation of the book as a whole, I am indebted to Kathryn Fraser and Haidee Wasson, who have been of invaluable assistance in tracking down references and citations.

Will Straw, Montreal, July 1997.

Pella, Palace of Alexandria. Mosaic of Dionysius and the panther (photo taken before restoration). Private collection of t'Serstevens.

What does man actually know about himself? Is he, indeed, ever able to perceive himself completely, as if laid out in a lighted display case? Does nature not conceal most things from him – even concerning his own body – in order to confine and lock him within a proud, deceptive consciousness, aloof from the coils of the bowels, the rapid flow of the bloodstream, and the intricate quivering of the fibres? She threw away the key. And woe to that fatal curiosity which might one day have the power to peer out and down through a crack in the chamber of consciousness and then suspect that man is sustained in the indifference of his ignorance by that which is pitiless, greedy, insatiable, and murderous – as if hanging in dreams on the back of a tiger.

Nietzsche, 'On Truth and Lies in a Nonmoral sense,' in *Philosophy and Truth: Selections from Nietzsche's Notebooks of the early 1870s*. Translated and edited by David Breazeale (Atlantic Highlands, N.J.: Humanities Press; Hassocks: Harvester, 1979), p. 80.

1

Marx – Black Magic

In The German Ideology, Marx has recourse to an
analogy which he declares is perfect for describing
both the process of inversion which is part of any
ideology and the necessity of this process: 'If in all
ideology men and their circumstances appear upside
down as in a *camera obscura*, this phenomenon arises
just as much from their historical life-process as the
inversion of objects on the retina does from their
physical life process.'[1]

This is analogy in the sense which Kant gives it:
'. . . a perfect similarity of two relations between quite
dissimilar things.'[2] It involves setting up a relationship
between a social phenomena and a physical phenomena thanks to a common feature which legitimates
the analogy: inversion. However, while, on the retina,
there occurs a spatial inversion, from bottom to top
or from top to bottom, in the case of the camera
obscura of ideology this inversion takes place in only
one direction (from bottom to top) and is to be
understood metaphorically.

A second metaphor clarifies the first and describes
the inversion of the inversion brought about by Marx:

1

'In direct contrast to German philosophy which descends from heaven to earth, here we ascend from earth to heaven.'[3] To move from an inversion between top and bottom to one between sky and earth is nevertheless, it would seem, to remain at the level of a purely spatial inversion. The second metaphor, however, introduces a supplementary religious connotation. There is a slight displacement: Marx draws attention to the privileged status of religious ideology as exemplary, even constitutive, of ideology as such. He notes, as well, that the ideological inversion is a hierarchical inversion which substitutes, for a real foundation, an imaginary one. The inversion of the inversion involves departing from 'real premises,' founded on real bases, the empirically observable 'material bases', and deriving, from these, those phantasmagorias which are ideological formations. The head should not be below but above, and it is not the sky but the earth which should serve as ground: it is men, of flesh and bone, men in their real activity, who should serve as points of departure, not their language or their representations, which are simple reflections and echos: 'That is to say [das heisst], we do not set out from what men say, imagine, conceive, nor from men as narrated, thought of, imagined, conceived, in order to arrive at men in the flesh. We set out from real, active men, and on the basis of their real life-process we demonstrate the development of the ideological reflexes and echoes of the life process.'[4]

2

'That is to say?' Will the language of science finally speak 'properly' of ideology, after having made use of metaphors and analogies for its didactic ends? Still, reflections and echos take us back once more to the camera obscura. All these specular metaphors imply the same postulate: the existence of an original meaning, of original sounds and light which would only secondarily reflect or reverberate. The 'real' and the 'true' would still preexist consciousness.[5] The history of sciences shows us that the camera obscura imposes itself as a model for vision in order to do away with that Euclidian conception according to which it is from the eye that emanates the luminous ray. The model of the camera obscura thus implies the existence of a 'given' which would offer itself as already inverted.[6] Thus, even when Marx seems to *want* to use his own, specific language, metaphors join together as system and weigh down upon him. This is a metaphorical constraint which warrants investigation.

The metaphor of reflection works to convey the sense that the autonomy of ideology is illusory. 'The phantoms formed in the human brain are also, necessarily, sublimates of their material life-process, which is empirically verifiable and bound to material premises. Morality, religion, metaphysics, all the rest of ideology and their corresponding forms of consciousness, thus no longer retain the semblance of independence. They have no history, no development; but men, developing their material production and their material intercourse, alter, along with this their real existence, their thinking and the products of their thinking.'[7]

> Its premises are men, not in any fantastic isolation or abstract definition . . .[8]

> When reality is depicted (*Darstellung*), philosophy as an independent branch of activity loses its medium of existence.[9]

Where, however, from within ideology, comes the illusion of independence? The camera obscura and other specular metaphors all imply a relationship to the real. Marx, too, is obliged to join to them the chemical metaphor of sublimation, which describes a process of idealization involving the volatilization of the constitutive elements; from here stem both the 'forgetting' of the processes of genesis and the illusion of independence. The process of sublimation accounts for the ethereal character of ideology, its fixation at the level of the clouds, its incapacity to come down to earth. Everything happens, therefore, as if the key to the dark chamber had been thrown away and the idea abandoned within the box, imprisoned, condemned to turn narcissistically around itself. The idea is a reflection cut off from its source, henceforth unable to engender anything but reflections of reflections, simulacra, fetishes.

Are the metaphors of the camera obscura and of sublimation compatible with each other? What is required for us to pass from a relationship of inversion to a sublimation or a fetishization? Does the requirement that we affix the metaphor of sublimation to the metaphor of the camera obscura not prove that the latter, taken on its own, remains overly ideological as a metaphor inasmuch as it is too specular? To describe ideology as a camera obscura – is this not to remain, as Marx reproaches Feuerbach, at the level of a speculative criticism, a criticism which sees religious relations as the transposition to the heavens of human relations – a cricism which, because it is speculative, is incapable of explaining the apparent autonomy of religion?

> Feuerbach starts out from the fact of religious self-alienation, the duplication of the world into a religious, imaginary world and a real one. His work consists in the dissolution of the religious world into its secular basis. He overlooks the fact that after completing his work, the chief thing still remains to be done. For the fact that the secular foundation lifts itself above itself and establishes itself in the clouds as an independent realm is only to be explained by the self-cleavage and self-contradictoriness of this secular basis. The latter must itself, therefore, first be understood in its contradiction and then, by the removal of the contradiction, revolutionized in practice. Thus, for instance, once the earthly family is discovered to be the secret of the holy family, the former must then itself be theoretically criticized and radically changed in practice.[10]

5

There is no point, then, in uncovering the family secrets hidden within the darkness of the chambers: the appearance of autonomy is explained, in the final analysis, 'by internal contradictions of the temporal base.'

The 'concept' of ideology, with all that links it to the Greek *eidos* and to the look,[11] thus remains speculative, Feuerbachian. The inversion of the inversion cannot, in fact, invert anything. Only the transformations of real contradictions are able to displace or resolve problems.

Are there then contradictions within Marx's 'text'? Is *The German Ideology* a more ideological text than the *Theses on Feuerbach*? Is Marx constrained, by his language, by his play of metaphors, to remain, no matter what he does, within ideology? In any case, there is an absence of homogeneity within what we think of as Marx's text: the insistence of specular images and the system of oppositions (theory/practice, real/imaginary, light/darkness) which are everywhere at play seem to mark this text metaphysically. But we find as well, in these same texts, what we require in order to deconstruct the notion of ideology and all that still remains of the ideological: the proliferation of metaphors which makes it possible to displace and reevaluate each one of them, the critique of the Fuerbachian critique of religion which warns us against a purely specular inversion; and finally, this other text, from *Capital*, which takes up the optical metaphor again, but in order to denounce its limits.

Marx – Black Magic

This text from *Capital*, on first glance, is not concerned with ideology, but with exchange value and its relation to use value. It should be referred to, then, with caution:

> Whence, then, arises the enigmatic character of the product of labour, so soon as it assumes the form of commodities? Clearly from the form itself. The equality of all sorts of human labour is expressed objectively by their products all being equal values; the measure of the expenditure of labour-power by the duration of that expenditure, takes the form of the quantity of value of the products of labour; and finally, the mutual relations of the producers, within which the social character of their labour affirms itself, take the form of a social relation between the products.

> A commodity is therefore a mysterious thing, simply because in it the social character of men's labour appears to them as an objective character stamped upon the product of that labour; because the relation of the producers to the sum total of their own labour is presented to them as a social relation, existing not between themselves, but between the products of labour. This is the reason why the products of labour become commodities, social things whose qualities are at the same time perceptible and imperceptible by the senses. In the same way the light from a object is

perceived by us not as the subjective excitation of our optic nerve, but as the objective form of something outside the eye itself. But, in the act of seeing, there is at all events, an actual passage of light from one thing to another, from the external object to the eye. There is a physical relation between physical things. But it is different with commodities. There, the existence of things *qua* commodities and the value-relation between the products of labour which stamp them as commodities, have absolutely no connexion with their physical properties and with the material relations arising therefrom. There it is a definite social relation between men, that assumes, in their eyes, the fantastic form of a relation between things. In order, therefore, to find an analogy, we must have recourse to the mist-enveloped regions of the religious world. In that world the productions of the human brain appear as independent things endowed with life, and entering into relation both with one another and the human race. So it is in the world of commodities with the product of men's hands. This I call the Fetishism that attaches itself to the products of labour, so soon as they are produced as commodities, and which is therefore inseparable from the production of commodities.[12]

In order to resolve the enigmatic character of the commodity, Marx has recourse to the religious analogy. Their commonality? That religious ideas, products of the human mind, and, like commodities, products of the human hand, give the illusion of being autonomous once cut off from the processes of their own genesis. The result, for the former, is their fixation in the heavens; for the latter, their phantasmagorical character. However, if religion is one form of ideology, it is also the form of every ideology. Only the religious illusion may found that of a perfect autonomy, characteristic of all ideology. It alone can legitimate the radical separation 'between heaven and earth,' between high and low; it alone may justify the hierarchical inversion effected by ideology.[13] To say that the fantastic character of the commodity is analogous to that of religion is to say that it is analogous, either to a specific ideological object or to every ideological object. What might be said of the relation between exchange value and use value should, therefore, hold true analogically for ideology. It is no accident that the same terms and metaphors turn up to describe both ideology and exchange value. We find the same metaphor of inversion, the same fetishistic character attributed to the one as to the other:

> The fetishistic character of the commodity and its secret. A commodity appears, at first sight, a very trivial thing and easily understood. Its analysis shows that it is, in reality, a queer thing, abounding in metaphysical subtleties and theological niceties. So far as it is a value in use, there is nothing mysterious about it, whether we consider it from the point of view that by its properties it is capable of satisfying human wants, or from the point that those properties are the product of human

9

labour. It is as clear as noon-day, that man, by his industry, changes the forms of the materials furnished by Nature, in such a way as to make them useful to him. The form of wood, for instance, is altered, by making a table out of it. Yet, for all that, the table continues to be that common, every-day thing, wood. But, so soon as it steps forth as a commodity, it is changed into something transcendent. It not only stands with its feet on the ground, but, in relation to all other commodities, it stands on its head, and evolves out of its wooden brain grotesque ideas, far more wonderful than 'table-turning' ever was.[14]

It is, in fact, a fantastic table which faces other commodities in a specular, narcissistic relationship. Exchange value causes the differences between commodities to disappear; each becomes the mirror of the other's value. 'The value of a commodity is reflected in the body of all other commodities as in a mirror.'[15] To cut commodities off from the social relations of labour, from 'reality', is, as within ideology, to leave room for specular relations: the reciprocal contemplation by commodities of each other, the engendering of ideas one from the other, the reflections of reflections. Swept up in vertigo, having lost its grounding, drunk, the table dances. It turns.[16] Should we say that, between exchange value and ideology, there exists a simple relationship of analogy? The only difference offered by Marx is that we are dealing with a product of the hands, in one case, with a

10

product of the mind, in the other. Is not this distinction itself, however, an ideological one? Might we not conclude that if the 'ratio cognoscendi' of exchange value is the religious analogy, the 'ratio essendi' of religion is the illusory autonomy of exchange value of which it is the simple reflection? It would suffice, then, to understand the material base, that is, to transform its contradictions, to make religion disappear. The reification of relations of production is 'a religion of daily life',[17] a spontaneous fantasmatic, a family romance, which is at the base of the religious phantasmagoria strictly speaking. Ideology is not the reflection of real relations but that of a world already transformed, enchanted. It is the reflection of a reflection, the phantasm of a phantasm.

If exchange value and ideology differ from each other only as the psychology of everyday life differs from a more systematic, more elaborated delirium, then there is no distinction in kind between them. The same processes are at the basis of one, as of the other, since, strictly speaking, one is the 'reply' to the other. Nor is it astounding to see Marx use the same metaphors to describe them. The metaphor of sublimation is used for exchange value and for ideology:

> Let us now consider the residue of each of these projects; it consists of the same unsubstantial reality in each, a mere congelation of homogenous human labour, of labour-power expanded without regard to the mode of its expenditure. All that these things now tell us is,

11

that human labour-power has been expended in their production, that human labour is embodied in them. When looked at as crystals of this social substance, common to them all, they are – Values.[18]

This, too, is an optical metaphor, but *Capital*, unlike *The German Ideology*, shows its limits: in the act of vision, we are dealing with a physical relation between physical things; in exchange value, the social relations of labour gives the illusion of a physical relation between things. This comparison is insufficient, however, and so the religious analogy is substituted for it. Marx seems to have 'forgotten' that, in *The German Ideology*, it was an optical analogy, that of the camera obscura, that he had used to describe ideology and, thus, religion. If the religious analogy is superior to the optic analogy, this is because the latter is not suitable for describing ideology. *Capital* prevents us from ever saying thereafter that, in ideology, everything takes place absolutely as if on the retina. The metaphor of the camera obscura is inadequate for speaking of ideological inversion. At the same time, the optical metaphor is used, in *Capital*, to describe the illusion of autonomy: 'In the same way the light from an object is perceived by us not as the subjective excitation of our optic nerve, but as the objective form of something outside the eye itself.'[19]

Although it produces the appearance of autonomy, the eye, nevertheless, does not elicit a fetishism of the object, because it does not bring about a hierarchical inversion. The fantastic character of exchange value requires another analogy.

In *The German Ideology*, therefore, the metaphor of the camera obscura seems appropriate for describing ideological inversion. Nevertheless, it must be married to the metaphor of sublimation in order that autonomy be accounted for. In *Capital*, the optical metaphor allows us to understand autonomy but not inversion, and so, indirectly, the camera obscura is denounced as an inadequate analogy. The use of the metaphor of the camera obscura shows a lack of elaboration in the notion of inversion; it is used, at one and the same time, in a spatial sense, in the sense of a hierarchical transformation of values, and to describe a qualitative transformation of the object.

THE ENCLOSED CHAMBER

The camera obscura, in the technical sense of the term, seems to me to be contaminated by more ideological, more unconscious connotations, carried simultaneously by the notion of camera/chamber and that of 'obscura.' In ideology, ideas are put under lock and key in a room, cut off from the real material base which alone can confer upon them light and truth. The dark chamber 'is a place where light can only enter through a hole an inch in diameter to which one applies a glass which, letting the rays from external objects pass onto the opposite wall, or onto a curtain held there, allows what is outside to be seen inside.' (Littré.)

This is Plato's cave; and, far outside, the sun.

Camera obscura: this was also, in certain monasteries, the place where monks disciplined themselves, a dark place where sexual prohibitions were transgressed, and where everything that was meant to be hidden took place. It it the very symbol of the veil. Ideology, the camera obscura, here takes on all those connotations which hold true equally for unconscious and mythical thought. Ideology represents real relationships veiled, under cover. It functions, not as a transparent copy obeying the laws of perspective, but, rather, as a simulacrum: it disguises, burlesques, blurs real relationships. To this, Marx opposes the values of clarity, light, transparency, truth, rationality. The camera obscura functions, not as a specific technical object whose effect is to present, in inverted form, real relationships, but, rather, as an apparatus for occultation, which plunges consciousness into darkness, evil and error, which makes it become dizzy and lose its balance. It is an apparatus which renders real relationships elusive and secret.

> Hence, when we bring the products of our labour into relation with each other as values, it is not because we see in these articles the material receptacles of homogenous human labour. Quite the contrary: whenever, by an exchange, we equate as values our different products, by that very act, we also equate as human labour, the different kinds of labour expended upon them. We are not aware of this, nevertheless we do it. Value,

therefore, does not stalk about with a label describing what it is. It is value, rather, that converts every product into a social hieroglyphic. Later on, we try to decipher the hieroglyphic, to get behind the secret of our own social products.[20]

When, therefore, Galiani says, 'Value is a relation between two persons' (...) he ought to have added: a relation between persons expressed as a relation between things.[21]

The determination of the magnitude of value by labour-time is therefore a secret, hidden under the apparent fluctuations in the relative values of commodities.[22]

The social relations of the individual producers, with regard both to their labor and to its products, are in this case perfectly simple and intelligible, and that with regard not only to production but also to distribution.[23]

And for a society based on the production of commodities, in which the producers in general enter into social relations with one another by treating their products as commodities and values, whereby they reduce their individual private labour to the standard of homogeneous human labour – for such a society, Christianity with its *cultus* of abstract man, more especially in its bourgeois developments, Protestantism, Deism, etc., is the most fitting form of religion.[24]

Those ancient social organisms of production are, as compared with bourgeois society, extremely simple and transparent ... the social relations within the sphere of material life, between man and man, and between man and Nature, are correspondingly narrow. This narrowness is reflected in the ancient worship of Nature, and in the other elements of the popular religions. The religious reflex of the real world can, in any case, only then finally vanish, when the practical relations of every-day life offer to man none but perfectly intelligible and reasonable relations with regard to his fellowmen and to Nature.[25]

The life-process of society, which is based on the process of material production, does not strip off its mystical veil until it is treated as production by freely associated men, and is consciously regulated by them in accordance with a settled plan. This, however, demands for society a certain material ground-work or set of conditions of existence which in their turn are the spontaneous product of a long and painful process of development.[26]

Some economists are misled by the fetishism inherent in commodities, or by the objective appearance of the social characteristics of labour.[27]

Whence arose the illusions of the monetary system?[28]

[Ricardo] has explained the apparent relation between objects, such as diamonds and pearls, in which relation they appear as exchange-values, and disclosed the true relation hidden behind the appearances, namely, their relation to each other as mere expressions of human labour.[29]

Thus, the camera obscura isolates consciousness, separates it from the real; enclosed, the latter contructs a sort of neoreality, analogous to that produced by psychotics. Marx characterizes this world as ghostly, fantastic, phantasmagorical or even fetishistic. The last term lends itself to being understood in its technical, psychoanalytic sense. For Freud, fetishism implies both the recognition and disavowal of reality and the constitution of a substitute: the fetish, the recognition and denial of castration, the perception that the mother's penis is missing, and the disavowal of this perception.[30] The camera obscura of ideology simultaneously maintains a relationship to the real (which it reflects in an inverted form) and occults, obscures it. The camera obscura functions like an unconscious which can, or cannot, accept the sight of this or that reality. What is it that ideology refuses to see? Who is refusing? What is missing, in the real, such that it cannot be recognized? The camera obscura is the unconscious of a class, of the dominant class which, in order to maintain its domination indefinitely, has an interest in hiding from itself the historical character of its domination, indeed all that is historical, the processes of genesis, the divisions of labour ... indeed, difference itself.

Thus, it would serve no purpose to lift the veil in order to make reality appear in its transparency; this would involve forgetting the possibility of hallucination, whether negative or positive, forgetting that transparency is itself a product of history and not something which precedes ideology. The model of the camera obscura might make Marx say what he never wished to say: on the one hand, because it is a mechanical model, it sheds no light on the relationship of ideology to desire; on the other hand, it presupposes an original truth, now obscured, secondarily, by being put in the chamber, a presence which will be inverted in representation. For Marx, however, the darkness is primary and cannot be overcome through theory, through a pure and simple unveiling. The apparatus bringing about this splitting is that of an originary, indestructible repression. There is no eye without its camera obscura, even that of science. If science had an eye.

THE CAMERA LUCIDA

For Marx, then, science is no longer either specular or speculative. Even if he dreams of passing from a camera obscura to a camera lucida, he declares that only practical transformations may – and then after a 'long and painful development' – bring about transparent and rational relationships. Scientific or theoretical progress cannot dissipate ideological phantasmagoria. These are as 'natural' and invariable

... as 'the atmosphere itself' which remained unaltered 'after the discovery by science of the component gases of air'.[31]

Clear meaning thus does not pre-exist ideological obscurity, and there is no 'truth' without a labour of transformation. Clarity comes only in the moment of the after-effect [après-coup] and is attained, not through the resolution of theoretical contradictions, but through a practical revolution. The camera obscura is never set right by a camera lucida.

Still, to characterize ideology as a dark chamber suggests nostalgia for a clear, transparent, luminous knowledge and implies that this is primary; even if science is no longer specular, speculative, a repetition, reflection or echo, its ideal remains that of a perfect eye, a pure retina.[32] Nevertheless, the recognition that every eye has its camera obscura does not disqualify the eye as a model of knowledge. In fact, that model is never really questioned by Marx. If every eye has a camera obscura, this should lead, it seems, to the generalization of the ideological and to the rendering as non-pertinent of the distinction between ideology and science. However, Marx maintains this distinction, even if, *at one and the same time*, he shows that ideology may never be set right by science; even if, for him, science has no eye. It is a question, then, of the complexity of Marx' gesture, of the heterogeneity of his text.[33] And the dividing line is no longer a simple 'break' in the middle of a 'corpus.'

The German Ideology, like *Capital*, rehearses a

19

system of traditional, mythical and ideological oppositions; and yet, these same texts enact displacements with which it is possible to undertake the work of deconstructing the system of oppositions on which they remain dependent.

2

Freud – The photographic apparatus

Although Marx speaks more of an ideological consciousness than a class unconscious, the camera obscura functions, for him, much in the manner of the unconscious. Explicitly and repeatedly, Freud calls on this metaphor in his description of the unconscious. However, like the science of his time, he substitutes for the model of the camera obscura that of the photographic apparatus. The difference between these two models is minimal, the physical image in one becoming a chemical impression in the other. Still, through the mediation of the notion of the negative, the theory of vision remains the same: to see is always to obtain a double. The usage and principle remain identical.

The photographic metaphor returns several times, replacing those of the screen and of the sieve which are to be found in the *Project for a Scientific Psychology*.[34] The *Three Essays on Sexuality* defines the neuroses as the negative of perversion.[35] A note specifies that, in the case of the perverse, the phantasm is *clearly* conscious.[36] Perversion is like a development of neurosis; it implies a passage from darkness to

21

light, or from the unconscious to consciousness. Freud's use of the model of the photographic apparatus is intended to show that all psychic phenomena necessarily pass first through an unconscious phase, through darkness and the negative, before acceding to consciousness, before developing within the clarity of the positive. However, it is possible that the negative will not be developed. The passage from darkness to light entails an ordeal, a test, and this is always a showdown of sorts. As well, Freud declares the photographic analogy to be crude and insufficient. To it, he adds other metaphors, making it clearly understood that, between the negative and positive phases, there intervene forces which enact a selection from among the negatives. The metaphor here is that of the watchman, the censor, present at the entrance to the dark antechamber, forbidding certain drives from entering into the clear room of consciousness.

> Unconsciousness is a regular and inevitable phase in the processes constituting our psychical activity: every psychical act begins as an unconscious one, and it may either remain so or go on developing into consciousness, according as it meets with resistance or not. The distinction between foreconscious and unconscious activity is not a primary one, but comes to be established after repulsion has sprung up. Only then the difference between foreconscious ideas, which can appear in consciousness and reappear at any moment, and unconscious ideas which cannot do so gains a theoretical as

well as a practical value. A rough but not inadequate analogy to this supposed relation of conscious to unconscious activity might be drawn from the field of ordinary photography. The first phase of the photograph is the 'negative': every photographic picture has to pass through the 'negative process': and some of these negatives which have held good in examination are admitted to the 'positive process' ending in the picture.[37]

Not every negative, however, necessarily becomes a positive; nor is it necessary that every unconscious mental process should turn into a conscious one. This may be advantageously expressed by saying that an individual process belongs to begin with to the system of the unconscious and can then, in certain circumstances, pass over into the system of the unconscious. (. . .) The crudest idea of these systems is the most convenient for us – a spatial one. Let us therefore compare the system of the unconscious to a large entrance hall, in which the mental impulses jostle one another like separate individuals. Adjoining this entrance hall is a second, narrower room – a kind of drawing-room – in which consciousness, too, resides. But on the threshold between these two rooms a watchman performs his function: he examines the different mental impulses, acts as a censor, and will not admit them into the drawing room if they displease him. (. . .) The impulses in the entrance hall of the unconscious are out of sight of the conscious,[38] which is in the other room; to begin with they must remain unconscious.

Now I know you will say that these ideas are both

crude; and, more than that, I know that they are incorrect, and, if I am not very much mistaken, I already have something better to take their place. Whether it will seem to you equally fantastic I cannot tell. They are preliminary working hypotheses [and] are not to be despised (...). I should like to assure you that these crude hypotheses of the two rooms, the watchman at the threshold between them and consciousness as a spectator at the end of the second room, must nevertheless be very far-reaching approximations to the real facts.'[39]

THE STEREOTYPE

The metaphor of the photographic negative persists in *Moses and Monotheism*.[40] Here, Freud uses it to describe the decisive influence of early childhood. The idea of the negative implies that an impression made may be retained without change, to be repeated within a image which will subsequently develop it. The metaphor is intended to show the constraining character of the past, and the compulsional force which determines its return, makes it dictate behavior, shape emotions, and so on. If the past repeats itself in this way, duplicating itself within representation, it is because the event has never been lived in the fullness of tis meaning, in the positivity of its presence: 'the psychic apparatus of the child was not yet completely receptive' to a certain number of impressions nor ready to endow them with meaning.

24

Counter-proof: Hoffman's declarations, in which he 'used to trace back the wealth of figures that put themselves at his disposal for his creative writings to the changing images and impressions which he had experienced during a journey of some weeks in post-chaise while he was still an infant at his mother's breast.'[41] Freud then concludes: 'What children have experienced at the age of two and have not understood, need never be remembered by them except in dreams; they may only come to know of it through psycho-analytic treatment.'[42]

In *Moses and Monotheism*, then, the metaphor of the photographic apparatus is not used for the exact same ends as in other texts. This latter usage allows us to reevaluate the sense of the image of the negative and to suggest that the Freudian text is, at the very least, ambivalent.

THE DEVELOPMENT OF THE NEGATIVE

In effect, whenever Freud puts a metaphor in play, he always acts with great caution: he multiplies the images, declares them crude, provisional, or uses them for purely didactic ends. He will correct one metaphor with another, even though it is spatial metaphors which seem to him the most apt for describing the psychic apparatus. Images – of the censor, of the guard, of the watchman – will complete those of the photographic apparatus, unable to express, on its own, the conflictual character of the psyche. The

25

camera obscura, a simple mechanical model, cannot give us a 'good' picture of the unconscious: it fails to show that there are forces with an interest in producing or perpetuating ideological inversion. Such a model, with its emphasis on the necessity of inversion and on its mechanical character, obscures the class struggle and the relationship to desire. The precautions Freud takes, the fact that he questions his own methodological use of metaphors, shows the limits of the optical analogy in Marx.

Despite everything, despite the scientific character of his approach, Freud's text nevertheless fails to avoid the traditional system of mythical and metaphysical oppositions: unconscious/conscious, dark/light, negative/positive. A negative proof is 'that which reproduces the model in inverted colours, the darks as light, the lights as dark. In order to obtain a positive proof, one applies the first negative drawing onto another sheet of paper possessed of the same properties and exposes the whole to light.' (Littré). But the term 'negative' has pejorative connotations: it is linked to darkness, to the antechamber, to the valet's backroom. As for consciousness, characterized by light, lucidity, the positive, it resides in a more noble place, the salon: it is the master. A text like this lends itself to the belief that psychism will submit to the same finality as the Hegelian dialectic: the passage from darkness to light. Photographic development would then suggest the development of the Spirit, becoming itself in the course of time, the positive taking over from the negative. Psychic time would therefore be linear: 1. the time of infancy, of the impression leaving a negative imprint; 2. the time of latency, the time of development or growth; 3. the time of the positive image, marked by the passage from darkness to light, from infancy to adulthood. The positive image, the double of the negative, implies that 'what is at the end is already there in the beginning.' Development adds nothing: it only enables the darkness to be made light.

In fact, even the first texts we have cited, but especially *Moses and Monotheism*, block such a Hegelian reading of Freud. In the psychic apparatus, the passage from negative to positive is neither necessary nor dialectical. It is possible that the development will never take place. Repression is originary, and there is always an irretrievable residue, something which will never have access to consciousness. The death drive, as a generalized economic principle, prevents us from confusing the negative in Freud with that in Hegel. What is more, when there is a passage into consciousness, it depends not on logical criteria, but on a selection involving conflicts between non-dialectizable forces. Finally, to pass from negative to positive is not to become conscious of a pre-existing meaning, light, or truth of a reason diverted from itself the better to be found, reappropriating itself in the course of its development. The passage to light takes place through a procedure which is not theoretical but practical: the analytic cure. As with Marx, only a transformation of the balance of forces leads to clarity. To pass from darkness to light is not, then, to rediscover a meaning already there, it is to construct a meaning which has never existed as such. There are limits to repetition inasmuch as full meaning has never been present. Repetition is originary. Hoffman's 'creations' are the substitute memories of a past which never took place, of a presence which never existed. Substitutive procedures, whether normal or pathological, are originary repetitions which allow us to construct, after the fact, *post festum,* the meaning of experience, but as a hypothetical construction.[43] Thus, the photographic metaphor contains within it all we need to undertake a metaphysical reading of Freud, but also, and at the same time, what we need to undo these clichés. Provided that we read these texts with caution, we can see that a metaphor, like a concept, is not 'metaphysical' in itself. Like that of Marx, Freud's text is heterogeneous.[44] It would seem, nonetheless, that the hypothesis of the death drive is that 'more interesting thing,' announced by Freud in the *Introduction to Psychoanalysis* , which would put an end to 'fantastic' metaphors. The theory of the death drive dispels, then, any recourse to metaphysics, even though, in Freud's own words, that theory was the most speculative that he had ever advanced.[45]

3

Nietzsche and the Painter's Chamber

THE KEYHOLE

The camera obscura turns up several times in Nietzsche. It would be dangerous to separate this image from other Nietzschean metaphors. Like Freud, Nietzsche multiplies his metaphors, using them to correct or complete each other; he joins unheard-of metaphors to others of long standing, for purposes which are no longer simply didactic but strategic. To isolate one metaphor would be to privilege it, to make believe that it lent itself more properly than another to expressing the proper or natural, to make of it the latter's servant. However, Nietzsche's generalization of metaphors blurs the opposition between the proper and the metaphorical and prevents us from making, of the metaphor, a simply didactic device.[46] With these precautions in mind, we note that, alongside the image of the camera obscura, we also find that of the door-keeper, the watchman stationed at the entrance to consciousness, charged with upholding and monitoring etiquette.[47] The dark chamber is set in relation to a system of forces which are themselves intended to establish a certain hierarchy among forces. It is, therefore, the metaphor for forgetting, for a forgetting

29

necessary to life. Nietzsche employs this metaphor by
playing on its mythical connotations and reining it in
as close as possible. The chamber of consciousness has
a key, and it would be dangerous to want to look
through the keyhole – dangerous and impertinent.
Woe to the curious! We must throw away the key.

This metaphorical play has the effect of revealing
all that the analogy of the camera obscura carries
with it of the sexual, and of showing the full impact
this analogy may have on the unconscious – which
may explain the persistence of this metaphor in texts
which are at first glance very different, and from a
period when the camera obscura had ceased to serve
as the model of vision.

LEONARDO'S CHAMBERS

In Nietzsche, the analogy of the camera obscura is no
longer based on the model of the photographic apparatus, nor on that of the eye. Rather, Nietzsche refers
to an eye whose dark chamber may not be mistaken
for a light chamber: the eye of the painter. This shift,
insignificant as it may seem, is an important one. Even
though, historically, the painter's camera obscura and
that which served as a model for vision are the same;
and even though, for a painter like Leonardo Da
Vinci, who was the first to build a model of the eye
based on the dark chamber, the camera obscura is a
means for accurately reproducing objects situated at a
certain distance; a tool for copying, even if the object

given in the camera obscura appears inverted, in accordance with the laws of perspective.

> *Proof that objects reach the eye*. If you look at the sun or some other luminous body and then shut your eyes you will see it again inside your eye for a long time. This is evidence that images enter into the eye.[48]

An experiment, showing how objects transmit their images or pictures, intersecting within the eye in the crystalline humour. This is shown when the images of illuminated objects penetrate into a very dark chamber by some small round hole. Then, you will receive these images on a white paper placed within this dark room and rather near to the hole, and you will see all the objects on the paper in their *true forms and colours*, but much smaller, and they will be upside down by reason of that very intersection. These images, being transmitted from a place illuminated by the sun, will seem actually painted on this paper which must be extremely thin and looked at from behind. And let the little perforation be made in a very thin plate of iron. (1: 142)

Everything that the eye sees through the small holes is seen by this eye upside down and known straight. (1: 144)

How objects on the right would not appear to be on the right to the visual organ if their images did not pass through two intersections. (1: 145)

For Leonardo, the painter must be a faithful mirror of the universe. His studies on perspective will enable him to attain the highest level of objectivity. The camera obscura is a means for becoming the transparent imitator of nature:

> The mind of the painter must resemble a mirror, which always takes the colour of the object if reflects and is occupied by the images of as many objects as are in front of it. Therefore you must know, O Painter! that you cannot be good if you are not universal master to represent by your art every kind of form produced by nature. And these you will not know how to do if you do not see them, and retain them in your mind. (1: 310)

> And since you can see that the mirror, by means of outlines, shadows, and lights, makes objects appear in relief, you, who have in your colours far stronger lights and shades than those in the mirror, can certainly, if you understand how to put them together well, make also your picture look like a natural scene reflected in a large mirror. (1: 320)

> That painting is most praiseworthy which conforms most to the object portrayed.

> Perspective is nothing else than seeing a place behind a pane of glass, quite transparent, on the surface of which the objects behind that glass are to be drawn.

These can be traced in pyramids to the point in the eye, and these pyramids are intersected on the glass plane. (1: 50)

The eye of the painter is the preeminently ideal eye. Which is not to say that it is passive: this mirror must become conscious of that which takes shape within it. It is by combining colours and shapes, in this way or that, that the painter renders his work similar to that of nature. Only bad or lazy painters are content with copying nature, looking at it 'through glass or transparent paper or veils' (1: 97), limiting themselves to the act of tracing. Those methods are to be used only to make the work easier, and to avoid deviation from the 'truthful imitation of a thing' (1: 97). The 'true' painter must be able to invent, to reproduce, via imagination and calculation, the effects of nature (1: 97).

To imitate nature, looking to discover the variety of forms which it has produced; to seek to capture the 'infinite causes that have never occurred in experience' (2: 240) — it is an eager quest, this yearning to peer into the most intimate of nature's nooks and crannies. On the pretext of a desire for objectivity, does the painter's camera obscura not send us to an entirely different dark chamber, a whole other cavern?

Unable to resist my eager desire and wanting to see the great multitude of the various and strange shapes made

by formative nature, and having wandered some distance among gloomy rocks, I came to the entrance of a
great cavern, in front of which I stood some time,
astonished and unaware of such a thing. Bending my
back into an arch I rested my tired hand on my knee
and held my right hand over my downcast and con-
tracted eyebrows: often bending first one way and then
the other, to see whether I could discover anything
inside, and this being forbidden by the deep darkness
within, and after having remained there some time,
two contrary emotions arise in me, fear and desire –
fear of the threatening dark cavern, desire to see ·
whether there were any marvelous thing within it.
(2: 324)

Wanting to know and to see; dreading, yet desiring
to see. The menacing cavern, the fear of being
engulfed within the belly of Nature and yet the desire
for the same.[49] Nature, the mother, can be frighten-
ing. Darkness is not always a means for reaching
transparency. After all, it stops one from seeing
whether or not the mother has the penis. Fetishism:
might the camera obscura, as an instrument of transparency, not be that fetish which serves to deny the
darkness of the other chamber and that which it
conceals? Might it not be the substitute penis offered
to the mother?[50]

Nietzsche and the Painter's Chamber

At the level of consciousness, then, the camera obscura is an instrument of transparency for the painter, and not only during the Renaissance. In the eighteenth century, a Dutchman, Gravesande, writes a treatise on perspective in which he devotes ten pages or so to describing the camera obscura and its uses in designing. He describes the workings of two machines, one of which may be carried about. The first is in the shape of a sedan chair; the second, that of a large box in which another, smaller box is to be placed. Gravesande provides the following description:

> A Camera Obscura is any dark place, in which outward objects exposed to Broad-Day-light, are represented upon paper, or any other white body.
>
> The way to represent objects in the Camera Obscura, is to make a small hole in that side thereof next to the objects, and place a convex glass therein, then if a sheet of paper be extended in the focus of the said glass, the objects will appear inverted upon the paper.[51]

Gravesande then goes on to state and demonstrate two theorems, which stress the fact that the camera obscura provides a true representation of objects:

Medusa, after Leonardo de Vinci. Ufficio, Florence.

35

Theorem I

The Camera Obscura gives the true representation of objects.

The figures represented in the Camera Obscura are form'd (as is demonstrated in Dioptricks) by rays which coming from all the points of the objects, pass through the centre of the glass: So that an eye placed in the said centre would perceive the objects by the said rays, which consequently by their intersection with a plane, must give the true representation of the objects. But the pyramid which the said rays forms without the Camera Obscura, is similar to that which they form, after having passed through the glass: therefore the rays which fall upon the paper in the Camera Obscura, likewise give the true representation of the objects thereon. *Which was to be demonstrated.*[52]

Gravesande then shows the usefulness of the camera obscura for truthfully representing the faces of men. One recognizes very distinctly, he says, persons of one's acquaintance.

Was Rousseau familiar with this text: he who, in preparing to paint, not his face but his soul, writes that he will place himself in a camera obscura so as to offer that soul to the reader unabashedly and in all its truth?[53] The recourse to the camera obscura allows Rousseau to distinguish himself from all those other writers who, in their books, turn themselves into flattering representations. Going far beyond literary and deceptive paintings, the camera obscura would restore the very presence of the soul in all its clarity and, with it, the presence of nature itself:

> If I want to produce a work written with care, like the others, I won't paint myself, I'll paint over myself. This is my portrait, not a book. I shall be working, as it were, in a camera obscura. No art is needed beyond that of tracing exactly the features that I observe there. I am decided, then, upon the style as on the things.... I will speak each thing as I feel it, as I see it, without reflection, without embarrassment, without getting bogged down in fine points.[54]

This is a unique and hitherto unrealized project. The camera obscura enables Rousseau to write a book, the *Confessions*, which is no longer a book but a painting, a portrait. It allows him to cast upon himself the point of view of God himself.

> I will be truthful; I will be so without reservation; I will tell all: the good, the evil; in the end, everything. I will comply rigorously with my title, and the most fearful among the devout will never undertake a better examination of their consciences than that for which I prepare myself; never will they lay before their confessors the innermost recesses of their souls more scrupulously than will I lay mine before the public.[55]

Rousseau places himself in the camera obscura because, in the absence of himself as author, others have painted of him the darkest of possible portraits, based on the mere reading of his writings. The camera obscura is a supplement meant to vindicate (*blanchir*) him, to bring a paternal support to his orphanly writing; to offer, on behalf of he who disclaims any apology, his apologies:

> With the most easy-going of airs they blackened me with kindness; in effusive friendship they rendered me hateful; by pitying me, they tore me apart. . . . Nothing was more unlike me than that picture; perhaps I was not better than it was, but I was different. In good and in evil I was rendered no justice. Since my name will endure among men, I wish that it no longer bear a fallacious reputation; I no longer wish . . . to be painted with features which are not my own.[56]

The camera obscura is that language [*langage*], as new as the project itself, which would make it possible to disguise nothing, to disclose all, down to the last detail, even at the risk of appearing impertinent, at the risk of being ridiculous and indecent. Only in this way might one find one's way amidst the chaos of contradictory feelings, amidst 'this bizarre and singular assemblage' which nevertheless constitutes a self.

What trifles, what miseries must I not disclose, into

what revolting, indecent, puerile and often ridiculous detail must I not enter so as to follow the thread of my secret inclinations...? Even as I blush at the mere thought of those things I must say, I know that hardened men will again treat as impertinence the humiliation of my most painful admissions: but I must make these admissions or disguise my true face.[57]

Rousseau is thus superior to those painters who seize upon the conspicuous features of character but show little concern for true resemblance; who, in any case, would not be able to see the inner model. He is superior, as well, to those who see the inner model but do not care to show it. He along is able to confront image and model; and he would see no difference between them. The metaphor of the camera obscura is thus given as a perfect model of passivity and objectivity. As the point of view of God, it is, in fact, the point of view of indecency. Wanting to see everything implies a frog's perspective.[58] Curiously, Rousseau uses the metaphor of the camera obscura without, at any point, taking account of perspectivist distortion. Is there not a denial going on here? To claim, so loudly and so often, that one wishes to conceal nothing: is this not the sign that one has something to hide? By placing virtue and vice on the same plane, out of a desire to be sincere, is one not seeking to better conceal the latter? Here, again, the camera obscura plays the role of a fetish. Indeed, Freud found that a fetish was all the more

durable the more it was 'doubly derived from contrary ideas.'[59] Here again, the camera obscura takes
us back to a whole other darkness. The use of the
metaphor of the camera obscura in Rousseau flows
from the entire system of metaphysical oppositions:
presence/representation, disguise/unveiling, truth/
error, obscurity/transparency, etc. We see, once again,
that when Marx and Freud take up this system for
their own purposes they are unable, in certain
respects, to avoid being caught within the same field,
even if certain shifts are effected: even if the stress is
now placed, not on transparency, but on obscurity;
not on objectivity, but on inversion. But, as Nietzsche
taught us, opposites belong to the same system.

DECENCY/INDECENCY

It is indeed Nietzsche (and after this necessary detour
we must return to him) who, in taking up the
pictorial metaphor of the camera obscura, generalizes
it. Each man has his camera obscura, his perspectivist
point of view. The camera obscura is never a camera
lucida, and in the use which Nietzsche makes of this
metaphor there is no nostalgia for clarity. Strategi-
cally, Nietzsche repeats this classical metaphor in
order, precisely, to denounce the illusion of transparency; to show that the latter is based in that indecent
point of view which makes one look at things from
bottom to top: the point of view of the weak.[60] The
generalization of the camera obscura is the generali-

zation of perspectivism. No eye is without its point of view, and none is passive, even that of science. That, too, is an artistic activity, albeit one which is unaware of itself as such. Contrary to what the model being used here would lead us to believe, neither art nor science capture within their chamber a world which would preexist them in all its truth: each constitutes its real on the basis of its singular, instinctive judgements. The generalization of the camera obscura makes it possible to erase the oppositions art/science, unconscious/conscious, darkness/light. If all is obscurity, then nothing is. Nietzschean deconstruction always passes through a phase of hierarchical reversal, with the generalization of one of two opposed terms. The effect of this generalization is to render irrelevant the use of either of two opposites. To generalize the camera obscura is, in short, to render it, as a metaphor, precarious, to denounce it as belonging to metaphysics. However, as Derrida has shown with respect to his own method of deconstruction – one very close to Nietzsche's – the first stage is that of a *paleonomy*, and that alone enables one to take hold of the older system.[61]

Moral for psychologists. Not to go in for backstairs psychology. Never to observe in order to observe! That gives a false perspective, leads to squinting and something forced and exaggerated. Experience as the *wish* to experience does not succeed. One *must* not eye oneself while having an experience; else the eye becomes 'an evil eye.' A born psychologist guards instinctively against seeing in order to see; the same is true of the born painter. He never works 'from nature,' he leaves it to his instinct, to his *camera obscura*, to shift through and express the 'case,' 'nature,' that which is 'experienced'. . . . Nature, estimated artistically, is no model. It exaggerates, it distorts, it leaves gaps. Nature is *chance*. To study 'from nature,' seems to me to be a bad sign: it betrays submission, weakness, fatalism; this lying in the dust before *petits faits* is unworthy of a *whole* artist. To see *what is* – that is the mark of another kind of spirit, the anti-artistic, the factual. One must know *who* one is.[62]

The metaphor of the camera obscura has as a corollary that of inversion. However, if everyone has a camera obscura, this does not mean that everyone sees the world as inverted. Why is there not a generalized inversion? What criteria can we use in speaking of an inverted point of view, if there is no perspective which offers real relationships in all their transparency, if science and truth are themselves the point of view of a certain kind of 'spirit' – that, precisely, of those who see truth upside down? 'And yet here truth is all topsy-turvy, which is particularly unsuitable for truth.'[63] The point of view which sees relations as inverted is that neither of error nor of illusion. It is that of a certain kind of mind – an anti-artistic one – which wants to see reality without veils, naked, from the point of view of indecency. Naked, in broad daylight, outside of the dark chamber of consciousness. It is the perspective of those who are unaware that, behind the veil, there is yet another veil. It is the symptomatic unawareness of the instincts' loss of virility. To seek the unveiling of truth is to reveal that one no longer knows how to get it on with women. That one doesn't know about – or doesn't want to know about – the differences between the sexes: fetishistic denial. The inverted point of view is that of a perverse judgement, by instincts neither strong enough nor fine enough to love appearance for appearance's sake. Or to love life or woman, without looking behind the veils, in feverish fear of castration, for a penis and a stable world to cling to.

> Supposing that Truth is a woman – what then? Is there not ground for suspecting that all philosophers, insofar as they have been dogmatists, have failed to understand women – that the terrible seriousness and clumsy inopportunity with which they have usually paid their addresses to Truth, have been unskilled and unseemly methods for winning a woman? Certainly she has never allowed herself to be won. We no longer believe that truth remains truth when the veils are withdrawn; we have lived too much to believe this. Today we consider it a matter of decency not to wish to see everything naked, not to be present at everything, or to understand and 'know' everything.[64]

'Is it true that God is present everywhere?' a little girl asked her mother; 'I think that's indecent' – a hint for philosophers! One should have more respect for the bashfulness with which nature has hidden behind riddles and iridescent uncertainties. Perhaps truth is a woman who has reasons for not letting us see her reasons? Perhaps her name is – to speak Greek – *Baubo*? ... Oh, those Greeks! They knew how to live. What is required for that is to stop courageously at the surface, the fold, the skin, to adore appearance, to believe in forms, tones, words, in the whole Olympus of appearance. Those Greeks were superficial – *out of profundity*.[65]

Baubo? She who succeeded in making Demeter laugh in spite of her unhappiness, by pulling up her skirts and letting Demeter see her belly?[66] Demeter, searching for her daughter, who had been kidnaped by Hades and taken into the dark underworld? Demeter, attached to her daughter as to a phallus? Is it not better to laugh than to cry at the loss of the object, or at castration? To laugh at appearances, rather than to deny them? Seek, you metaphysicians, to unveil the world and you will find still another veil, a painting: on Baubo's stomach was the figure of a head, that of Iacchus.[67]

Demeter, Baubo, Core: a story of women. Demeter, goddess of fertility who, under the weight of her sadness, acts like a sterile, castrated woman searching after knowledge: 'When a woman has scholarly inclinations there is generally something wrong with her sexual nature. Barrenness itself conduces to a certain virility of taste.'[68] The legend specifies that, for nine days and nights, Demeter ceased drinking, eating, bathing and adorning herself. For a woman, the search for truth is an assault on her own decency, a disavowal of sexual difference.[69]

Nevertheless, Dionysus is naked, without shame. He is naked because he is not ashamed of his own appearance, he has no need of metaphysical finery as of so many fetishes.[70] Dionysus' nudity is not that of revelation, of an unveiling of truth, but the uncloaked affirmation of appearance. To make oneself naked is to show, against any future denial, that there is nothing to hide. Dionysus is the equivocal god *par excellence*, doubly sexed like life itself. He is like Woman, 'whose mastery includes the knowledge of how to seem': he is that God 'who does not say a word or cast a glance in which there is no consideration and ulterior enticement.' Like a man, he is sufficiently strong, profound and good-looking to risk nakedness.[71] He is the Greek God, the undecidable God, for whom surface and depth, man and woman are false oppositions. Dionysus' nudity is his most solid mask, that with which he seduces Ariadne. Nudity is that fetish which would put an end to all fetishisms. To live is to assert virility and femininity at the same time, in their difference and their unity.

With Nietzsche, we are thus far from the dream of – or the nostalgia for – transparency. For him, the aim of the metaphor of the camera obscura is to show that the values of clarity, or of truth as an unveiling, and all those values bound up with them, are symptoms of an illness – of a loss of virility and a fetishistic denial.

From the point of view of decency, science and ideology, as Marx conceived them, are cut from the same cloth. It is by borrowing from metaphysics a metaphor in which the system of oppositions characteristic of that metaphysics is implicated, and by then generalizing it, that Nietzsche is able to displace traditional values, while at the same time subjecting them to a symptomatic and differential reading. After all, while everyone has their camera obscura, it does not follow that all such cameras are equally good. That of the painter – or, at any rate, that of a certain kind of painter – is preferable to that of science, because the former does not pass off its darkness as clarity. Ultimately, it is the point of view of decency – which is the same as that of health – and not that of truth, which allows one to distinguish between one chamber and another, and to introduce a difference between them. What the texts of Marx and Freud had begun to unhinge receives its most decisive blow with Nietzsche. The Nietzschean dark chamber, without a key, should put an end to all false clarities, all obscurantisms.

THE BLINDING GLARE

The point of view of decency, the artistic point of view which allows man not to die from truth: 'Art rests upon the imprecision of sight. . . . Its principal means is *to omit, to not see and not hear.*'[72] Wanting to see, no matter what the cost, wanting to uncover the secrets of nature, risking the unavowable truth that there is no truth – all this leaves one open, like the intrepid Oedipus, to becoming the unhappiest of men, to losing one's sight[73] from having cast a 'glance into the abyss.'[74] Is the camera obscura not that blinding which strikes us all so as to save us from an eventual loss of sight, a preventative remedy which allows us to remain serene? In the Nietzschean text, we might say that it comes, like a screen-memory, to block and replace that 'light-picture [*Lichtbild*] which, after our glance into the abyss, healing nature holds up to our eyes,'[75] as discussed in *The Birth of Tragedy* with reference to Oedipus and the Sophoclean hero.

> The language of the Sophoclean hero, for instance, surprises us so much by its Apollonian precision and clarity, that we at once think we see into the innermost recesses of their being, not a little astounded that the way thereto is so short. But let us, for the moment, disregard the character of the hero which rises to the surface and grows visible – and which at bottom is nothing but the light-picture cast on a dark wall, that is, appearance through and through. Instead, let us enter into the myth which is projected in these bright mirrorings. We shall suddenly experience a phenomenon which has an inverse relation to one familiar in optics. When, after trying hard to look straight at the sun, we turn away blinded, we have dark-coloured

spots before our eyes as restoratives, so to speak: while, reversing the colours, those light-picture phenomena of the Sophoclean hero – in short, the Apollonian of the mask – are the inevitable consequences of a glance into the secret and terrible things of nature. They are shining spots intended to heal the eye which dire night has seared.[76]

This look, cast into the horrible interior of nature, into the belly of the mother, can only remind us of Leonardo's fear and desire on seeing 'the threatening dark cavern.' The 'luminous reflections' evoke the serene works Leonardo produced with the aid of the camera obscura, just as Nietzsche's undecidable Dionysus reminds us of Leonardo's androgynous figures. And Nietzsche did have a certain nostalgia for the Renaissance.

Are Leonardo, Rousseau, and Nietzsche not all linked by the same homosexual structure, by the same desire, the same fear of seeing and knowing, by the same look cast upon an unbearable truth? Have not all three been petrified [*médusés*] by the mother?

The camera obscura is that magical apparatus which serves to placate horror: it functions as an *apotropaeon*. Freud reminds us that the proliferation of symbols of the penis signifies castration and the defense against castration.[77] Is Nietzsche's generalization of the camera obscura not, ultimately, a more effective (and more ambiguous) remedy than its use as a device for tracing and transparency?

4

The Ox's Eye – Descartes and the Ideological After-Effect

Before it was the metaphor for objective knowledge, as with Rousseau, or of perspectivist knowledge, as in Marx and Nietzsche, or of the unconscious, as in Freud, the camera obscura was a technical apparatus which served as a model of vision. At the very moment when Marx employs it as a metaphor for ideological inversion, science begins to think that the problem of inversion is a false one.[78] Moreover, from 1840 on, it is known that light produces modifications in the sensitive layer of the retina (that of the cones and rods), whose effect is a nervous influx toward the brain which acts within it in a photo-chemical manner; the eye thus comes to be likened to a photographic apparatus, and the physical image is now a chemical impression. Freud, with his metaphor of the negative, was more in tune with the scientific models of his time. Leaving aside Marx's (ideological) backwardness with respect to science, his use of the camera obscura metaphor is like that of all those who employed it as a model, inasmuch as it implies a confusion between the retinal image and the retinal impression, between the retinal impression and the object perceived. The retinal 'image' is an effect, a means necessary to seeing but not itself intended to be seen. Moreover, and paradoxically, as long as the camera obscura remained a model for vision it in no way disqualified the eye as a model for knowledge; such a model excluded any empiricist conception of perception.[79] The eye was always a good eye, for it was always already set right by the intellect. The inversion of the inversion was immanent to perception, and the eye was always the eye of a geometrist. If we take the Marxist analogy seriously, then ideology should set itself right on its own, or, at the very least, should always be set right by the activity of the mind. When Marx substitutes practical transformation for the mind's eye, or for a theoretical science, he breaks with his own historical model. Because of all the displacements which Marx enacts with respect to metaphysics, the metaphor of the camera obscura cannot be a good model for him, and the analogy cannot be a perfect one.

A counter-example is Descartes, who takes the camera obscura as a model of vision and undertakes a sectioning to show that perspectivist images exist at the back of the eye, and who neither disqualifies the eye as a model for knowledge nor ends up with a perspectivist conception of knowledge and of perception. Descartes eliminates the problem of inversion, since, if there are images at the back of the eye, the eye will not see such images. If, indeed, we see through the intermediary of luminous rays, then the analogy of the blind person's cane makes it clear that we must renounce any correspondence between the image and the object, between the object and the idea:[80]

> Thus you can clearly see that in order to perceive, the mind need not contemplate any images resembling the things that it senses. But this makes it no less true that the objects we look at do imprint very perfect images on the back of our eyes. Some people have very ingeniously explained this already, by comparison with the images that appear in a chamber, when having it completely closed except for a single hole, and having put in front of this hole a glass in the form of a lens, we stretch behind, at a specific distance, a white cloth on which the light that comes from the objects outside forms these images. For they say that this chamber represents the eye; this hole, the pupil; this lens, the crystalline humour, or rather, all those parts of the eye which cause some refraction; and this cloth, the interior membrane, which is composed of the extremities of the optic nerve.... But you will be even more certain of this if, taking the eye of a newly deceased man, or, for want of that, of an ox or some other large animal, you carefully cut through to the back the three membranes which enclose it.... Then, having covered it over with some white body ... you will see there, not perhaps without admiration and pleasure, a picture which will represent in natural perspective all the objects which will be outside it.[81]

Descartes distinguishes between the object seen, the internal organ (the optic nerve and the brain), the external organ (all the transparent parts of the eye) and all the intermediary parts between the brain and the object. The mind cannot do without the eye in order to see, but it is the mind that sees. Features (colours, shapes, distances, position, light, size) are details that the mind could not acquire from another organ, but they result either from the union of mind and body (for light and colour) or from a calculation. Shape results from a knowledge of the position of the different parts of the object, and doesn't involve any resemblance to pictures at the base of the eye. Because images on the retina are perspectivist, Descartes concludes that there is no resemblance between object and image. It is the mind that sees, and not the eye, and the mind is consciousness without point of view. At the same time, errors are of the mind, and it is possible to devise a science of perspectivist illusion.[82] The idea is thus not the reflection of the object, whether inverted or not. Vision involves an estimation [*est un calcul*], and one must become blind in order to know.[83]

In this way, the model of the camera obscura may lead to a non-perspectivist conception of knowledge, and work against the idea of knowledge as reflection. The idea is a product of the mind, which does not contradict the fact that elsewhere, for Descartes, the most perfect knowledge, rational intuition, is received as light from God.[84]

Descartes and the Ideological After-Effect

And so we turn to Descartes, who shows us that the use made of the camera obscura metaphor in the nineteenth century – as an image of the unconscious, of inversion, of perspectivism – is not a necessary consequence of the model itself. A metaphor such as this resists the evolution of science. That is, it operates above all through its mythical significations, and through its impact on the unconscious.[85]

Notes

1. Karl Marx and Friedrich Engels, *The German Ideology* (parts I and III). Translated and edited by R. Pascal, New York: International Publishers, 1947, p. 14.
2. Immanuel Kant, *Prolegomena*. Translated by Peter G. Lucas, Manchester: Manchester University Press, 1953, p. 125.
3. *The German Ideology*, p. 14.
4. *The German Ideology*, p. 14.
5. This is not to say that, for Marx, the real would be immutable nor that, by the real, he means nature as a pure abstraction, cut off from any relationship to man. Against Feuerbach, he shows that 'nature' is itself a product of history. However, at each step, the real, as 'material base' of human life, is the foundation of the ideology derived from it:

> Feuerbach speaks in particular of the perception of natural science; he mentions secrets which are disclosed only to the eye of the physicist and chemist; but where would natural science be without industry and commerce? Even this 'pure' natural science is provided with an aim, as with its material, only

through trade and industry, through the sensuous activity of men. So much is this activity, this unceasing sensuous labour and creation, this production, the basis of the whole sensuous world as it now exists, that, were it interrupted only for a year, Feuerbach would not only find an enormous change in the natural world but would very soon find that the whole world of men and his own perceptive faculty, nay his own existence, were missing. Of course, in all this the priority of external nature remains unassailed. *The German Ideology*, p. 36.

6. At the end of the Middle Ages, Euclidian notions are abandoned in the wake of Alhazen's work on optics, as divulged by Vitelio and R. Bacon. A number of empirical experiences are invoked: after having looked at the sun, if one closes one's eyes, one continues to see the solar disc for a certain time, which would be impossible if the ray emanated from the eye. Said eye, therefore, must be the recipient of rays coming from the outside. The impression of light persists within it as a weakened echo. To the objection already made to the εἴδωλα (how might the εἴδωλα of a mountain penetrate the orifice of a pupil), Alhazen responded that we must break down the surface of objects into a series of points, each of which would be the origin of a luminous ray. After it passes through the pupil, there is a recomposition of the object, with the proviso that the activity of the intellect comes to fill in the gaps and recompose the whole. While we represent

this phenomenon to ourselves as the projection of points, the rays which penetrate, crossed, into the pupil, give an inverted image.

Leonardo de Vinci, a reader of Vitelio, is the first to have constructed an eye on the model of the camera obscura (see above, page 32). He was the precursor of all that followed, but we must await Kepler to find the idea that the image takes an inverted form on the retina. Scheiner the Elder, then Descartes (see *La lettre du père Mersenne* of March 31, 1638 and *The Dioptricks* V and VI) do experiments enabling them to directly observe the image inverted upon the retina of an animal. In 1666, Mariotte throws these results into question by discovering, on the retina, a blind spot; he concludes that the image forms itself on a choroid. This conclusion was unnecessary but, without it, it would have been necessary to renounce the model of the camera obscura and accept, once more, the eye as origin of light.

The problem of inversion, and of the place of inversion, preoccupied science until 1826 or so. Wagner, in his article on 'seeing' in the dictionary of physiology, writes that we may only become aware of inversion through optical research, and that, inasmuch as we see everything in inverted form, the order is not changed: we see everything relatively. For the same reasons, Hermoltz and Muller, around 1866, no longer attach any importance to the phenomenon of inversion: inasmuch as natural consciousness is not even aware of the existence of the retina, it *a fortiori* knows nothing of the images which form upon it.

(We owe most of this information to the course given by M.G. Canguilhem at the Sorbonne in 1957. We thank him here.)

7. *The German Ideology*, pp. 14–15.
8. *The German Ideology*, p. 15.
9. *The German Ideology*, p. 15.
10. Karl Marx, 'Theses on Feuerbach,' reprinted in Friedreich Engels *Ludwig Feuerbach and the Outcome of Classical German Philosophy*. Translated and edited by C.P. Dutt, New York: International Publishers, 1941, p. 83.
11. J. Derrida, *Margins of Philosophy*. Translated by Alan Bass, Chicago: University of Chicago Press, 1982, p. 254.
12. Karl Marx, *Capital*, vol. 1. Translated by Samuel Moore and Edward Aveling, edited by Friedrich Engels, New York: International Publishers, 1967, pp. 71–2.
13. Nietzsche, as well, puts religion at the base of the 'inversion' of values. It is the priests who, by the transformation of the aristocratic judgement good/bad into the judgement pure/impure, found the radical, obsessive separation between the sensory and the intelligible, the sky and the earth, etc. See, in particular, *The Genealogy of Morals*, trans. Walter Kaufmann (New York: Vintage Books, 1967), essay I, Section 6, pp. 31–3; and our *Nietzsche and Metaphor*, trans. Duncan Large (London: Athlone Press, 1993; and Stan-

ford, California: Stanford University Press, 1993), pp. 51–8.

14. *Capital*, vol. 1, p. 71.

15. See Jean-Jacques Goux, 'Marc et l'inscription du travail,' *Tel Quel*, 35, 1968, pp. 64–89; and 'Nusmatiques (11),' *Tel Quel*, 36, 1969, pp. 64–74.

16. See also *Capital*, vol. III 'It is an enchanted, perverted, topsy-turvy world, in which Monsieur le Capital and Madame la Terre do their ghost-walking as social characters and at the same time directly as mere things.' Translated by Samuel Moore and Edward Aveling, edited by Friedrich Engels, New York: International Publishers, 1967, p. 830.

17. *Capital*, continuation of the previously cited text. 'It is the great merit of classical economy to have destroyed this false appearance and illusion, this mutual independence and ossification of the various social elements of wealth, this personification of things and conversion of production relations into entities, this religion of everyday life' (p. 830).

18. *Capital*, vol. 1, p. 38.

19. *Capital*, vol. 1, p. 72.

20. *Capital*, vol. 1, p. 74.

21. *Capital*, vol. 1, p. 74, note 1.

22. *Capital*, vol. 1, p. 75.

23. *Capital*, vol. 1, p. 79.

24. *Capital*, vol. 1, p. 79.

25. *Capital*, vol. 1, pp. 79–80.

26. *Capital*, vol. 1, p. 80.

27. *Capital*, vol. 1, p. 82.

28. *Capital*, vol. 1, p. 82.

29. *Capital*, vol. 1, p. 83, note 3.

30. See 'Fetishism' (1927), in Sigmund Freud, *Standard Edition of the Complete Psychological Works of Sigmund Freud*, vol. XXI, edited by, and translated under the direction of James Strachey, London: The Hogarth Press, 1961, pp. 152–7. Henceforth referred to as *Standard Edition*.

31. *Capital*. vol. 1, no. 1, p. 74.

32. This expression, as well as that of the camera obscura, are used by Valéry in *Degas Dance Drawing*: 'They did away with Subject matter, and in a short time, reduced all the intellectual concerns about art to a few discussions on texture or the color of shadows. The brain became a mere retina . . .' (p. 23).

> He [Degas] was contrasting what he called the 'setting', the literal representation of objects with what he meant by 'drawing.' He referred to that particular charge brought about by an artist's way of seeing and executing a subject, as against the exact rendering; as for instance in contrast to the camera [*chambre claire*]. This kind of 'personal error' meant that the labor of rendering an object by line and shadow could be called 'art'. The camera, which I substitute now for the 'setting', made it possible to begin working at any point without even looking at the ensemble and to ignore the relations between line and plane. There was no need of transforming the thing 'seen' into a thing

'lived', or an act committed by 'someone.' (...) There exist certain draughtsmen possessing the precision and accuracy of the camera, whose merit one cannot deny. (...) They are the exact counterpart of real 'artists' (pp. 55–6). Paul Valéry, *Degas Dance Drawing*, translated by Helen Burlin, New York: Lear Publishers, 1948.

Chambre claire: 'An optical instrument, which, used in drawing, alows one to see at the same time the objects being drawn and the paper.' (Littre)

33. Because of the complexity of Marx's gesture, we cannot simply apply, to him, Dominique Lecourt's conclusions concerning the metaphor of reflection in Lenin. Cf. Lecourt, *Une crise et son enjeu* (Paris: Maspero, 1973). Lecourt believes that the metaphor of reflection needs to be 'reduced', that is, detached from the image of the mirror that it seems, logically, to conjure up. Reflection, as Lenin understood it, should be seen as a 'mirrorless reflection' (p. 47) because it takes shape within a historical *process* of the acquisition of knowledges. The 'reflection' is not the passive inscription of some fact into a mind which receives it. Rather, the reflection designates an (active) *practice* of appropriation of the external world by thought (p. 43). The reflection is *approximative*. The reflection thesis (as opposed to any theory of knowledge) breaks with the theoretical space of philosophies of reflection.

So, while it is true that, in Marx, science is no longer theoretical, and that transparency and rationality are historical acquisitions, the model of the mirror remains in the form of the *camera obscura,* even if the reflection is always a reflection of a reflection. It cannot be said that, in Marx, the theory of reflection is a systematic decomposition of the phantasm of the mirror (p. 43). Ideology – indeed, the very notion of ideology – refers to such explicitly. Even if Marx tries to render the classical scheme of reflection more complex and to displace it, he continues to depend on it.

34. 'The sense-organs act not only as Q-screens, like all nerve-ending apparatuses, but also as sieves; for they allow the stimulus through from only certain processes with a particular period.' Freud, 'Project for a Scientific Psychology' [1895], *Standard Edition*, vol. I, 1966, p. 310.

35. Freud, 'Three Essays on Sexuality' (1905) in *Standard Edition*, vol. VII, 1953, pp. 165–7.

36. 'The contents of the clearly conscious phantasies of perverts (which in favourable circumstances can be transformed into manifest behaviour), of the delusional fears of paranoics (which are projected in a hostile sense on to other people) and of the unconscious phantasies of hysterics (which psychoanalysis reveals behind their symptoms) – all of these coincide with one another even down to their details.' Freud, 'Three Essays on Sexuality' (1905) in *Standard Edition*, vol. VII, 1953, p. 165, note 2.

37. Sigmund Freud, 'A Note on the Unconscious' [1912] in *Standard Edition,* 1958, vol. XII, p. 264.

38. On the conscious as sight, and the persistence of this image within the metaphysical tradition, see Jacques Derrida, *Margins of Philosophy*, p. 284.

39. Freud, 'General Theory of the Neuroses: Resistance and Repression' [1916–1917), *Standard Edition*, vol. XVI, pp. 295–6.

40. Freud, 'General Theory of the Neuroses: Resistance and Repression' [1916–1917), *Standard Edition*, vol. XVI, pp. 124–6.

41. Freud, 'Moses and Monotheism (III): The Return of the Repressed' [1939], *Standard Edition*, vol. XXIII, p. 126.

42. Freud, 'Moses and Monotheism,' p. 126.

43. See our *Enfance de l'Art*, (Payot, 1970), English translation *The Childhood of Art: An Interpretation of Freud's Aesthetics*, trans. Winifred Woodhull, New York: Columbia University Press, 1988, especially Chapter III.

44. Another example of this heterogeneity: the metaphor of *arousal* for describing the return of the repressed. In his study of Jensen's *Gradiva*, Freud denounces Jensen's use of this metaphor: '"Arouses," however, is certainly not the right description.' Freud, 'Delusions and Dreams in Jensen's Gradiva' [1907] *Standard Edition*, vol. IX, p. 47. The criticism of this notion intervenes at precisely the moment when Freud opposes a philosophical and etymological understanding of the unconscious. The latter consider consciousness as a point of departure, and establish, between the unconscious and the unconscious, a

simple difference of intensity. The Unconscious, then, is the latent, the dormant, that which Freud will call the preconscious. The metaphor of arousal or awakening thus has the effect of confusing the preconscious with the unconscious or even the repressed. However, several pages later, Freud takes up this metaphor twice on his own account: 'No mental forces are significant unless they possess the characteristic of aroused feelings' (p. 49). 'But as we have insisted with admiration, the author has not failed to show us how the arousing of the repressed erotism came precisely from the field of the instruments that served to bring about the repression' (p. 49). Despite himself, then, Freud seems to yield to a metaphorical constraint, such that to speak of 'a text by Freud' as of a text of any other author, no longer makes sense. To the point, even, where it seems no longer relevant to know if Freud uses that metaphor 'voluntarily or involuntarily' so soon after criticizing it.

45. See Freud, 'Beyond the Pleasure Principle' (1920), *Standard Edition*, 1955, vol. XVIII, pp. 7–66.

46. See my *Nietzsche et la métaphore*, Paris: Payot, 1972; English translation, *Nietzsche and Metaphor* trans. Duncan Large, London: The Athlone Press, 1993.

47. See Nietzsche, *The Genealogy of Morals*, trans. Walter Kaufmann, vol. 2, no. 1, New York: Vintage Books, 1967, pp. 57–8: 'To close the doors and windows of consciousness for a time; to remain undisturbed by the noise and struggle of our underworld of utility organs

working with and against one another; a little quiet-
ness; a little *tabula rasa* of the consciousness, to make
room for new things, above all for the nobler functions
and functionaries, for regulation, foreign, premedita-
tion (for our organism is an oligarchy) – that is the
purpose of active forgetfulness, which is like a door-
keeper, a preserver of psychic order, repose, and
etiquette'; see also 'Human, All Too Human,' Pt. 1,
trans Helen Zimmern, in *The Complete Works of
Friedrich Nietzsche*, vol. 6, New York: Russell and
Russell, 1964, p. 98: 'How little moral would the
world look without this forgetfulness! A poet might
say that God had placed forgetfulness as door-keeper
in the temple of human dignity.'

48. Jean Paul Richter, ed. *The Literary Works of Leonardo
da Vinci*, 2 vols, London: Phaidon, 1970, 1: 132. [This
translation is modified slightly to correspond with the
French. Unless otherwise stated, quotations from Leonardo da Vinci are from this edition, and references
provided in the text.]

49. In the story of the black-faced giant, 'horrible and
terrifying to look upon,' who caused 'the sky to be
overcast and the earth to tremble,' who left men no
hope but to take refuge in 'tiny holes and subterranean
caverns,' Da Vinci writes: 'I know not what to say or
do, for everywhere I seem to find myself swimming
with bend heat within the mighty throat and remaining indistinguishable in death, buried within the huge
belly.' *Codex Atlanticus*, trans. Edward MacCurdy, vol.
2, London: Jonathan Cape, 1956, pp. 403–4. The

horrible head of the giant may recall that of Medusa. There exists, in the Uffizi Gallery in Florence, a Medusa's head after Leonardo da Vinci. It would be interesting as well to consult his study for the head of Leda, whose hair is very serpentoid (Windsor Castle, Royal Library). This may be linked to the importance of rocks throughout his painted works, as backgrounds to the radiant heads of women. It is regrettable that Freud analyzed none of these texts.

50. This interpretation is not the only possible one. I acknowledge that Leonardo's research is inscribed within the cultural field of the Renaissance.

51. William-James Gravesande, *An Essay on Perspective*. Translated from the French by E. Stone, London: J. Senex, 1724, p. 103.

52. *An Essay on Perspective*, pp. 103–4.

53. [Starobinski writes: 'In Rousseau's time the camera obscura, which placed the art of portraiture within the reach of everyone, was a highly complex apparatus. Curio shops housed bulky advanced models, actually rooms that the painter entered in order to trace the image of the model, which was projected onto ground glass plates by a series of lenses and mirrors. The obediant hand almost passively traced the profile and shadows of the image. Then came Daguerre, who sensitized the plates with silver salts, completing the transformation of the camera into an automaton, in which images recorded themselves. That is the truth Rousseau believed he had achieved in speaking of himself. Before his own image he

wished to be as neutral, as mechanically faithful, as a camera.' Jean Starobinski, *The Living Eye*, trans. Arthur Goldhammer, Cambridge: Harvard University Press, 1989, p. 62.]

54. *Ebauches des Confessions*, vol. 1, Paris: Pléiade, 1969, p. 1154. The Confessions themselves do not take up this metaphor, but in his forward to the reader [not included in English editions] Rousseau writes: 'Here is the only portrait of a man, painted exactly according to nature and in all truthfulness which exists and will probably ever exist.'

55. *Ibid*, p. 1153.

56. *Ibid*, pp. 1152–3; see as well 1151: 'My books traveled through cities while their author traveled only through forests. Everyone read me, everyone criticized me, everyone spoke about me, but in my absence; I was as far from discourse as from men; I knew nothing of what they said. Each person imagined me in their fantasies, without fear that the original would turn up to refute them. There was one Rousseau in high society, and another in retirement who bore no resemblance to him whatsoever.'

57. *Ibid*, p. 1153. On the will to transparency and the desire for presence in Rousseau, see Jean Starobinski, *Jean-Jacques Rousseau: Transparency and Obstruction*, trans. Arthur Goldhammer, Chicago: University of Chicago Press, 1988), and Jacques Derrida, *Of Grammatology*, trans. Gayatri Chakravorty Spivak, Baltimore and London: The John Hopkins University Press, 1976. Starobinski devotes several pages to the

metaphor of the camera obscura in Rousseau in *The Living Eye*, pp. 14–77. It is our hope to add our own contribution to the remarkable readings by these two authors.

58. The frog's perspective is that which sees things from bottom to top, distorted. It produces a flattening of figures such that they appear shortened and squashed.

59. Freud, 'Fetishism' [1927], *Standard Edition,* vol. 21, 1961, p. 157.

60. We may recall that, for Freud, 'the foot or shoe owes its preference as a fetish – or a part of it – to the circumstances that the inquisitive boy peered at the woman's genitals from below, from her legs up.' 'Fetishism,' p. 155.

61. [For Derrida, the question posed by paleonomy is the following: 'what, then, is the strategic necessity that requires the occasional maintenance of an *old name* in order to launch a new concept?'] Jacques Derrida, *Positions*, trans. Alan Bass, Chicago: University of Chicago Press, 1981, p. 71.

62. Nietzsche, 'The Twilight of the Gods,' *The Portable Nietzsche*, ed. and trans. Walter Kaufmann, New York: The Viking Press, 1954, p. 517.

63. *Human, All Too Human*, p. 144; see also 'The Antichrist,' trans. Walter Kaufmann, in *The Portable Nietzsche*, p. 575: 'For truth has been stood on its head when the conscious advocate of nothingness and negation is accepted as the representative of "truth"'; and on page 576: 'Wherever theologians' instinct extends, *value judgements* have been stood on their

head and the concepts of "true" and "false" are necessarily reversed.'

64. 'Preface,' *Beyond Good and Evil*, trans. Walter Kaufmann, New York: Random House, 1966, p. xv.

65. 'Preface for the Second Edition,' *The Gay Science*, trans. Walter Kaufmann, New York: Random House, 1974, p. 38.

66. The role of Baubo is sometimes attributed to Iambe.

67. Iacchus was the child of Demeter. He was always an unobtrusive, obscure divinity sometimes identified with Dionysus. The scorched earth of Priene allows us to consider Baubo as the equivalent of a living *koilia* (a Greek word for the female sexual organ). Baubo's gesture reminds Demeter of the possibility she retains of being fertile. The 'obscene' gesture is a magical act for bringing about the fertility of the earth (see Salomon Reinach, *Cultures, mythes, religion*, vol. 4). Unless, that is, the figure on the belly was analogous to that of the Medusa. Reinach recounts other legends taken from Greek, Irish and Japanese contexts in which the fact of a woman lifting her skirts provokes either laughter or horror. Did Baubo not invite Demeter to go and frighten Hades? Baubo was Demeter's wet nurse. [In translating these passages, I have been guided at various points by Tracy B. Strong's translation of a related article by Kofman. See 'Baubo: Theological Perversion and Fetishism,' in *Nietzsche's New Seas*, eds Michael Allen Gillespie and Tracy B. Strong, Chicago and London: The University of Chicago Press, 1988, pp. 175–202.]

68. *Beyond Good and Evil*, p. 86.

69. '*Among women*: Truth? Oh, you don't know truth! Is it not an attempt to assassinate all our *pudeurs*?' *Twilight of the Gods,* p. 468; see also *Beyond Good and Evil*, p. 86: 'Comparing man and woman generally, one may say that woman would not have the genius for adornment, if she has not the instinct for the *secondary* role.'

70. 'The term "fetish" has undergone a curious semantic distortion. Today it refers to a force, a supernatural property of the object.... But originally it signified exactly the opposite: a fabrication, an artifact, a labour of appearance and signs. It appeared in France in the seventeenth century, coming from the Portuguese *fetiço*, meaning "artificial," which itself derives from the Latin *factitius*.... From the same root (*facio, facticius*) as *fetiço* comes the Spanish *afeitar*: "to paint, to adorn, to embellish", and *afeite*: "preparation, ornamentation, cosmetics," as well as the French *feint* and the Spanish *hechar*, "to do, to make" (whence *hechizo*, "artificial, feigned, dummy").' Jean Baudrillard, 'Fetishism and Ideology: The Semiological Reduction,' in *Towards a Critique of the Political Economy of the Sign*, trans. Charles Levin, St. Louis: Telos Press, 1981, p. 91.

71. *Beyond Good and Evil*, 235–6; on the question of nudity, see Kofman, *Nietzsche and Metaphor*, Chapter 4.

72. *Le livre du philosophe*, vol. 1, Paris: Aubier-Flammarion, 1969, paragraphs 54, 55.

73. *Le livre du philosophe*, vol. 1, paragraph 87; see also *Beyond Good and Evil*, pp. 160–1.
74. Nietzsche, *The Birth of Tragedy and the Case of Wagner*, trans. Walter Kaufmann, New York: Vintage Books, 1967, Section 9, p. 68.
75. Ibid. The term *Lichtbild* also refers to a photograph.
76. Ibid, pp. 220–1. Bernard Pautrat, in his fine *Versions du soleil*, Paris: Le Seuil, 1971, also cites this text (p. 144). This book as a whole, while not employing the metaphor of the camera obscura, nevertheless sheds light on the relationship between the questions of truth and of fetishism.
77. Freud, 'Medusa's Head' (1922) *Standard Edition*, 18: pp. 273–4.
78. See above, note 6.
79. This didn't prevent an empiricist philosopher like Locke himself from using the metaphor of the camera obscura. Perhaps Marx was familiar with this text: 'For methinks the understanding is not much unlike a closet wholly shut from light, with only some little opening left to let in external visible resemblances or ideas of things without: would the pictures coming into such a dark room but stay there, and lie so orderly as to be found upon occasion, it would very much resemble the understanding of a man, in reference to all objects of sight, and the ideas of them.' John Locke, *An Essay Concerning Human Understanding*, Oxford: Clarendon Press, 1924, book 2, chapter 11, p. 91.
80. The analogy of the blind man's cane is introduced in

the First Discourse of the 'Optics,' p. 67. The sensations transmitted to the blind man's hand as the cane encounters objects are likened to those transmitted to the eye by the passage of light emitted from luminous bodies. (Translator's note.)

81. René Descartes, 'Optics,' Fifth Discourse, in *Discourse on Method: Optics, Geometry, and Meteorology*, trans. Paul J. Olscamp, Indianapolis, New York and Kansas City: Bobbs-Merrill, 1965, pp. 91, 93: see also the Fourth Discourse, p. 89, where Descartes shows that the perfection of an image depends on it not resembling the original, offering as examples signs, words and perspective: and p. 90: 'These engravings ... are often better represented by ovals than by other circles; and squares by diamonds rather than by other squares; and so for all other shapes. So that often, in order to be more perfect as images and to represent an object better, they must not resemble it.'

82. '[H]ere again I would have you consider the reasons why [vision] occasionally deceives us. First of all, it is the mind which sees, not the eye; and it can see immediately only through the intervention of the brain. This is why madmen and those who are asleep often see, or think that they see, various objects which, in spite of this, are not actually before their eyes; that is, when certain vapors, disturbing the brain, dispose those of its parts which are usually used for sight in the same way as would these objects if they were present.' 'Optics,' Sixth Discourse, pp. 107–8.

83. The preface to the 'Principles of Philosophy' shows

that 'living without philosophy is just having the eyes closed without trying to open them.' In the *Philosophical Works of Descartes*, vol. 1, trans. Elizabeth S. Haldane and G.R.T. Rose, London: Cambridge University Press, 1967, p. 204.

84. See Rule III of the 'Rules for the Direction of the Mind,' in *The Philosophical Works of Descartes*, 1: pp. 7–8.

85. An earlier version of this text was presented to Jacques Derrida's seminar on religion and philosophy at the Ecole Normale Supérieure, in a film screening room, another camera obscura.

We would like to express our thanks to Jacques Derrida. We are indebted to him, in particular, for having suggested that, in Marx, religion is the very form of all ideology.

In *Camera Obscura* Sarah Kofman refers in passing to 'An Essay on Perspective' by the Dutch mathematician and physicist Willem Jakob S. Gravesande, 1688–1742. The essay was published in an English translation in London in 1724. Kofman cites Gravesande as a possible source for Rousseau's invocation of the camera obscura as a model for his intended truthful representation of himself in the *Confessions*. While the reference to Gravesande in Kofman's text is brief, she included a full translation of the 'Essay' in the French edition *Camera obscure de l'ideologie*. The text of the 1724 translation given below retains the

original phrasing and grammar while transposing eighteenth century typographical and orthographical elements
into their present-day form.

(Translator's note)

The Use of the Camera Obscura in Designing

William-James Gravesande, from Gravesande, *An Essay on Perspective*. Translated from the French by E. Stone, London: J. Senex, 1724.

DEFINITION

1. A Camera Obscura is any dark place, in which outward objects exposed to Broad-Day-light, are represented upon paper, or any other white body.

The way to represent objects in the Camera Obscura, is to make a small hole in that side thereof next to the objects, and place a convex glass therein, then if a sheet of paper be extended in the focus of the said glass, the objects will appear inverted upon the paper.

THEOREM I

2. The Camera Obscura gives the true representation of objects.

The figures represented in the Camera Obscura are formed (as is demonstrated in *Dioptricks*) by rays which coming from all the points of the objects, pass through the centre of the glass: So that an eye placed in the said centre would perceive the objects by the said rays, which consequently by their intersection with a plane, must give the true representation of the objects. But the pyramid which the said rays forms without the Camera Obscura, is similar to that which they form, after having passed through the glass: therefore the rays which fall upon the paper in the Camera Obscura, likewise give the true representation of the objects thereon. *Which was to be demonstrated.*

These objects appear inverted, because the rays cross each other in passing through the glass; those coming from above going below, etc.

THEOREM II

3. The reflection which the rays of light suffer upon a plain mirror or speculum, before they fall upon a convex glass, no-wise deforms the representation of objects.

This is evident: for the speculum reflects the rays in the same order as it receives them.

Now to show the use that may be drawn from the Camera Obscura in designing, I shall here lay down the description and use of two machines, which I use for this end.

The Use of the Camera Obscura in Designing

4. This machine is something in figure of a chair (such as people are carried in) the back part of the top is rounded, and its foreside P2 swells out in the middle: vide Fig. 1, which represents the machine, the side whereof opposite to the door is supposed to be raised up, that so its inside may be seen.

5. The board A within-side, serves as a table, and turns upon two iron-pins, going into the wood of the foreside of the machine, and is sustained by two small chains, that, so the said table may be lifted up; and therefore one may more conveniently go in at the door in the side of the machine.

6. There are two tin-tubes bent at each end ... placed in the furniture, near the back-side of the machine, each having one end without the machine. These tubes serve to give air to persons shut up in the machine, yet so, that no light may enter through them.

7. At the places c, c, c, c, on the outside of the back-part of the machine, are four Iron-staples, in which slide two wooden rulers DE, DE, about 3 inches broad, having two other thin rulers going through holes made at their tops, at the places D, D, to which thin rulers the board F is fixed; and so by this means the said board may be vertically moved backwards or forwards.

8. On the top of the machine, there is a board about 15 inches long, and 9 inches broad, having a

77

Camera Obscura

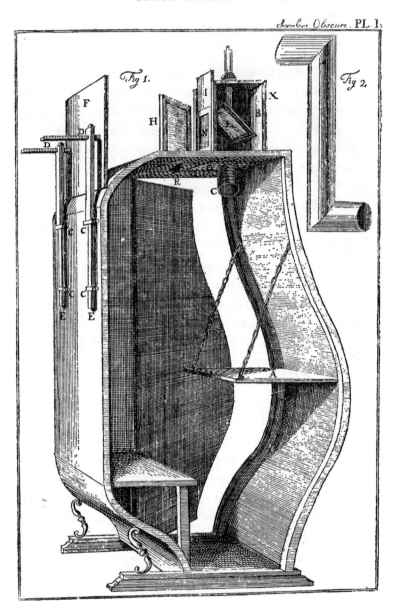

hole PMOQ quite through it, about 9 or 10 inches long, and four inches broad.

9. Upon the aforesaid board are fixed two Dovetail's rulers, between which another board slides of the same length as that, and whole breadth is about 6 inches. In the middle of this second board is a round hole about three inches diameter, hollowed into a female screw, in which is fitted a cylinder about four inches long, which carries the convex glass; of which more hereafter.

10. The figure X is a square box about 7 or 8 inches broad, and 10 in height, which slides upon the plain board mentioned in No. 8. The side b serving as a door, is next to the fore-side of the machine, as it appears in the Figure 3, and the back-side thereof hath in it a square opening N, each side being about four inches in length, which may be shut by the little board I, sliding between two rulers.

11. Over the said square opening, there is a slit parallel to the horizon, going along the whole breadth of the backside of the box; through which slit, a little mirror or looking-glass is to be put into the box, whose two sides may slide between two rulers so placed, that the polished side of the glass being turned towards the door B, may make an angle of 112½ degrees, with the horizon. Note, this disposition of the looking glass could not well be represented in the figure.

12. The afore-mentioned Mirror hath a small iron place, on the middle of that side which is without the

Box (when the said looking glass is in the disposition
mentioned in No. 11) being the base of a screw
fastened to the middle thereof, that of the looking
glass may be fixed upright (as appears per figure) in
any place H upon the top of the machine, and
vertically turn all ways; and this is done by putting
the screw through a hole made in the plain board of
no. 9 and through a slit made for this end in the
plain board of no. 8, and then fixing it with the nut
R. Now when the mirror is taken from this situation,
the said slit is shut by a small board sliding between
two little rulers within the machine. As to the slit
mentioned, no. 11, it is partly shut by the little board
I, when the aperture N is opened, and the two ends
thereof remaining opened, are shut by two small
rulers.

13. There are two iron staples on one side of the
box, like those which are on the backside of the
machine; in which a ruler going several inches out
behind the box X may slide, having a hole at its end,
through which the above-mentioned screw may pass,
and so the mirror H be fixed to any inclination before
the aperture N.

14. Besides the mirror H, there is another lesser
one, L, fastened near its middle to a ruler going out
through the middle of the top of the box. This ruler
may screw on, and serves to raise or lower the mirror
fastened to it, so that it may be fixed to all angles of
inclination.

REMARKS

If the tubes mentioned in no. 6 be not thought sufficient for giving air to the machine, a small pair of bellows may be put under the seat, which may be blown by one's foot. And by this means the air within the machine may be continually removed; for the bellows driving the air out of the machine, obliges the external air to enter through the tubes therein.

USE OF THE MACHINE

Problem I

15. To represent objects in their natural disposition.

When objects are to be represented within the machine, we extend a sheet of paper upon the Table A; or, which is better, we lay a sheet of paper upon another board, we lay a sheet of paper upon another board, so that it spreads beyond the edges of the board; then we squeeze the said paper and board into a frame, so that it be fixed therein by means of two dove-tailed rulers. This being done, we place a convex glass in the cylinder C, which screws into the top of the machine, having its focal length nearly equal to the height of the top of the machine above the table: then we open the aperture N at the back-part of the box, upon the machine; and incline the mirror L, so as to make an angle of 45 deg. with the horizon, when objects are to be represented for the perpendicular picture. Then, if the Mirror H be taken away, as also the board F, together with the two rulers D E and D E, we shall perceive the representation upon the sheet of paper on the table A, of all objects, whole rays falling upon the looking glass L, can be thereby reflected upon the convex glass, which convex glass must be raised or lowered, by means of the screw about the Cylinder carrying it, until the said objects appear entirely distinct.

16. When the same objects are required to be represented for the inclined picture, the looking glass L must have half the inclination we would give to the picture.

17. When the said objects are to be represented upon the picture being parallel, the aperture N must be shut, and the door B opened; then the mirror H must be raised to the top of the box, in putting it in a situation parallel to the horizon. This disposition of the machine may serve when one is upon a balcony, or some other high place, to design a *parterre* underneath.

18. If we have a mind to design a statue standing in a place something elevated, and it is required to be so represented, as to be painted against a ceiling; the backside of the machine must be turned towards the statue, and the box X so turned, that the door B may face the statue; then, the door being opened, the looking glass L must

be placed vertically, with its polished side towards the statue; and the box moved backwards or forwards; or else the looking glass raised or lowered, until the rays proceeding from the statue may be reflected by the mirror upon the convex glass. When these alterations of the box, or mirror, are not sufficient to throw the rays upon the convex glass, the whole machine must be removed backwards or forwards.

Demonstration

Concerning the before-mentioned inclination of the mirrors

19. In order to demonstrate, that the mirror L hath been conveniently inclined, we need only prove, that the reflected rays fall upon the Table A under the same angle, as the direct rays do upon a plane, having the same situation as one would give to the picture.

Now let AB be a ray falling from a point of some object upon the mirror GH, and from thence is reflected in the point a upon the table of the machine: We are to demonstrate, that if the line DI be drawn, making an angle with F E equal to the inclination of the picture; that is, if the angle DIE be the double of the angle DFI; I say, we are to demonstrate, that the angle BaF is equal to the angle BCD.

The angle DIE, by construction, is the double of the angle DFI; and consequently this last angle is equal to the angle IDF; and since the angle of incidence CBD is equal to the angle of reflection a BF, the triangle BCD is similar to the triangle F a B: Whence it follows, that the angle BaF is equal to the angle BCD. *Which was to be demonstrated.*

20. Concerning what has been said of the picture being parallel, it must be observed, that in the precedent demonstration, the angle of inclination of the picture in this demonstration is measured next to the objects; and if this angle be diminished till it becomes nothing, we shall have a picture parallel to the horizon underneath the eye. But, by the demonstration, the inclination of the mirror being half the inclination of the picture, it follows, that the inclination of the mirror is also equal to nothing, and consequently it ought to be likewise parallel to the horizon. In the same manner we demonstrate, that the looking glass must be vertically situated, when we consider the picture parallel above the eye: For to give this situation to the picture, the angle of the inclination of the picture measured next to the objects, must be augmented till it be 180 degrees, whose half 90 degrees is consequently the inclination of the mirror.

Problem II

22. *To represent objects, so that what appears on the right hand, ought to be on the left.*

23. Having placed the Box X, in the situation as per figure, the Door B must be opened, and the

Aperture N shut; then putting the Mirror H in the disposition mentioned in Number 11, raise up the Mirror L towards the top of the box; and incline it towards the first mirror, in such manner that it makes an angle with the horizon of 22½ degrees; that is, that the top of the machine, after a double reflection, appears vertical in the Mirror H.

24. Now if objects are to be represented for the picture inclined, the Mirror L must make an angle with the horizon, equal to half the inclination of the picture less 1/4 of a right angle. This angle is found exactly enough for practice, by inclining the Mirror L, until the representation of the top of the machine, after a double reflection, appears in the other mirror under an angle with the horizon, equal to the inclination one would give the picture. Note, if the inclination of the picture be lesser than 1/4 of 90 degrees, the Looking-Glass L must not be inclined towards the other, as is directed, but the contrary way, in making the angle of the inclination of the looking glass, equal to the difference of the inclination of the picture, and 1/4 of 90 degrees.

25. When the objects are to be represented for a parallel picture, the Looking Glass L must be placed in the disposition of no. 15, and the Looking-Glass Hl in that mentioned, no. 13, by inclining it towards the horizon, under an angle of 45 degrees; the polished side thereof facing downwards, when the picture is supposed underneath the eye; and upwards, when it is supposed above the eye.

26. This disposition of the machine may be likewise useful for inclined pictures, making very small angles with the horizon; in which case, the inclination of one of the looking glasses must be diminished, by half of the inclination of the picture.

27. *A Demonstration of the Inclination of the Mirrors.*

We have mentioned that for a perpendicular picture, one of the mirrors must make an angle of 112½ degrees with the horizon; and the other L, must be inclined towards the first, and make an angle of 22½ degrees with the horizon. Let MN and GH be two mirrors in the before-mentioned situation; we are to demonstrate, that if the Ray AB is parallel to the horizon, after being reflected in B and C, it ought to fall perpendicularly upon the machine. The angle ABN is 112½ degrees; and consequently the angle ABM, and its equal, the angle of reflection CBG are each 67½ degrees. The angle BPQ is the complement of the angle NBA, plus the angle PQB, which is 22½ degrees; whence the angle BPQ is 45 degrees. Again, the angle PCB is the complement of the two angles C B P and BPC to 180 degrees; and consequently it is 67½ degrees, which is the fame as its equal, the angle QCa of reflection. And reckoning after the same manner, the angle CRQ of the triangle RCQ is a right one. *Which was to be demonstrated*.

28. It is not absolutely necessary to give the mirrors the aforesaid inclinations; for the angle ABN may be

assumed at pleasure, from which must be taken an angle of 135 degrees, to have the inclination of the mirror GH. Nevertheless, the angles we have determined, are the most advantageous for a perpendicular picture.

29. When a picture is inclined, and makes the angle DIA with the horizon, the mirror M N must keep its situation, and the angle CQR is equal to half the angle DIA, less 1/4 of a right angle: Then I say, the angle FaC, or its equal CRQ, will be equal to the angle BID. Now the angle PBQ, is 112½ degrees; whence the angle B PQ, which is the complement of PBQ, and PQB to two right angles, is 90 degrees, less the half of the angle DIA: Wherefore because NBC is 67½ the angle BCP, and its equal RCQ, is 22½ plus ½ of DIA. Now if the angle RQC be added to this angle, their sum will be equal to the angle DIA; whence it follows, that the Angle CRQ is equal to DIR. *Which was to be demonstrated.*

30. If the angle RBN be altered, and it be called a, the angle DIA, b and the right angle d; then the angle CQR = d + 1/2b − a.

31. When a picture is parallel, it appears manifest, the mirrors GH and MN being each inclined under an angle of 45 degrees, that a ray, which is perpendicular to the horizon, likewise falls, after a double reflection, perpendicularly upon the Table A.

Problem IV.

32. To represent objects, which are round about the machine, and make them appear erect to the person seated within the same.

The backside of the machine must be turned towards the sun, and the objects behind the same represented by one reflection only; then their appearance will always be clearer, although they be in the shade, than the appearance of the objects, on the other sides of the machine, which cannot be perceived unless by a double reflection.

33. The objects that are on the right and left of the machine, may be represented by means of the mirror H, but the said mirror must be covered with a Pasteboard Case, having two apertures therein; the one next to the objects, and the other next to the aperture N, of the box X. The reason of our using this precaution is, because when the mirror is not covered at all, it reflects the rays of light coming sideways upon the mirror L, which being again reflected by the said mirror L, and going through the convex glass, extremely weakens the representation.

34. The objects before the machine are represented according to nos. 22, and 28.

Problem IV.

35. *To represent pictures or prints.*

If we have a mind to represent pictures and prints, they must be fastened against the board F on that side, regarding the back of the machine, which must be so turned, that the pictures be exposed to the sun. Then they are represented in this situation as the other objects, but with this difference, that the convex glass in the Cylinder C must be changed: For if prints are required to have their true bigness, the focal distance of the convex glass must be equal to half the height of the machine above the table; that is, equal to half AC. Again, if the said pictures or prints are required to be represented greater than they really are, the focal distance of the convex glass must still be lesser. And if, on the contrary, they are to be represented lesser than they really are, the focal length of the glass must be greater than the length AC. Moreover, the proper distance whereat the pictures or prints must be placed, may be found in sliding the board F backwards or forwards, until they distinctly appear within the machine. This distance also may be determined by the following proportion:

As the machine's height above the table, less the glass' focal length, is to the height of the machine above the table, so is the glass' focal length to the distance of the figure from the glass.

Note, the said distance of the convex glass from the figure, is measured by a ray, proceeding from the figure parallel to the horizon, which is perpendicularly reflected upon the convex glass, by the mirror. Note, moreover, that when we have a mind to place the figures out beyond the back-side of the machine, they must be fastened against the side F of the board, which must be so turned, that the said side be next to the aperture N.

37. Remarks concerning the representation of persons' faces.

It is certainly very curious and useful to design persons faces to the life; which by this machine, may be very well done in miniature: For if the face of any known person be thus represented, by only looking at the appearance, we may very readily know whose face it is, when at the same time the appearance of the whole person will not take up half an inch upon the paper on the table: But it is very difficult to represent a face distinctly as big as the life; for when we would represent a face in its natural bigness, such a convex glass as is mentioned in no. 35 must be used, and the face placed where the Board F is. But the said face which then appears distinct enough, that so the person whereof it is not the representation may thereby be known, hath not its lineaments sufficiently enough represented, as to be followed by a painter as they ought, in order to keep the true resemblance. The reason of this is, that the lineaments appear lively and distinct within the machine, when the re-union of the rays proceeding from a given point in the face, happens exactly upon the paper in one point only: But the least distance that one point is more than another from the convex glass, (when the distance of the face from the glass is so final, as it must be to represent it in its natural bigness) so alters the place of the said re-union, that for different parts of the face, those places of reunion will differ about two inches and a half. Whence it is no wonder that all the lineaments be not represented as could be wished, since in all distances chosen, there will be always a great many rays, whose re-union will fall above an inch besides the paper. The confusion arising from this diversity, though not being very distinguishable by the eye, yet is prejudicial, and hinders our getting the exact resemblance of the face. We have observed this, in order to give an exact idea of the goodness of this machine, in equally shewing wherein it may be really useful, and wherein its apparent usefulness is subject to an error rather discovered by experience than reason.

38. We must not forget in all the precedent problems, to examine the aperture the convex glass ought to have; for although we cannot reduce this aperture to a fixed measure, yet it is proper to observe the following remarks. 1. The convex glass may commonly have the same aperture, as we would give a perspective glass, having the said glass for its object glass. 2. When objects are very much enlightened, the said aperture must be lessened; and contrariwise,

when they are exposed to a weaker light, it must be made greater; and when any representation is to be copied, the convex glass must have the least aperture possible; but yet with this caution, that the light coming into the machine, must not be too much extenuated. From the same observations it is manifest, that we ought to be provided with several round pieces of tin or thin brass, having round holes of different bignesses therein, in order to give a necessary aperture to the glass; or holes of different bignesses may be made in a long thin piece of brass which may hide upon the convex glass; or else, we may use a round plate, having holes of different bignesses therein, which turning about its Centre, may bring any desired hole for the glass' aperture.

A DESCRIPTION OF THE SECOND MACHINE

39. This machine is a kind of box, the side ACGB being open, whose breadth BD, and height AB, are equal, each being about 18 inches: its greatest width FB, is 10 inches, and the side EP is sloping, so that AE is but about 6 inches.

40. The frame G slides at the bottom of the said box, in which the paper is fastened.

41. There is a round hole in the middle of the top of the box, in which the cylinder carrying the convex glass screws.

42. The two sticks HI and LM, slide in four little iron staples fixed to the inside of the top of

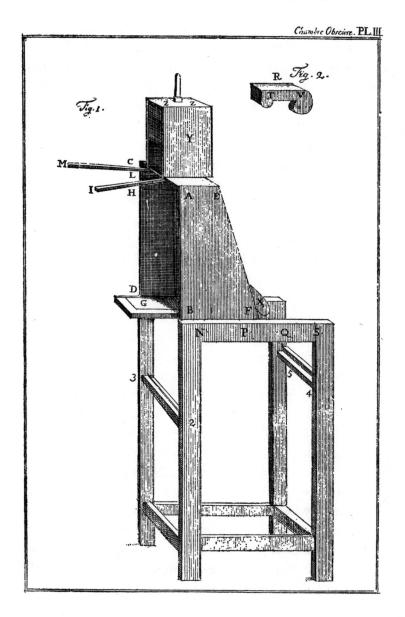

the box, like those mentioned in no. 7. These sticks come about two feet without the box, and the distance of their extremities I and M, is equal, or something greater than the length of the Box. Their use is to hang a black cloth upon, which is fastened to the three sides, BA, AC and CD, of the opening of the box, that so the box may be darkened, when objects are to be represented upon the paper in the frame G.

43. There are two pieces of wood serving to sustain the box upon its support or foot. One of these pieces may be fastened to one side of the support, and the other to the other side thereof, by means of four iron pins, two of which go through the holes N and P in the side of the support, and the holes T and V in the piece R, and the other two in like manner, through holes made in the other side of the support, and the other piece, when we have mind the bottom of the box should be parallel to the horizon; but when the box is to be a little inclined, that pin going through the Hole P, must be put through the Hole O, in the Piece R. Understand the same of the other piece.

44. We are sometimes obliged to let the box forwarder on its support, and this is done, in using the holes Q and S, instead of N and P. It is likewise something necessary to incline the box a little backwards; which may be done, by putting the pin in S, into the hole X, made in a piece of wood fastened to the back-side of the box, and the correspondent pin on the other side, into another hole made on the other side of the said piece.

45. The Box T slides upon the top of the machine, and is like that already described, but with this difference only, that it is lesser. On the top of the box are two little staples Z Z, in which a ruler slides, having a mirror fastened to it, in the manner as is mentioned in no. 13, and so by this means the said mirror may be put in the same situation, as that in the figure of the first machine it hath in H.

46. When we have a mind to remove this machine from one place to another, we lay the Box BEC upon the cross pieces 2, 3, 4, 5, with its opening ABC upwards; then we put the little Box T, the ruler and mirror (mentioned in no. 13), the black cloth, and the two sticks ML and IH, all into the said great box; and afterwards partly cover it by the Frame G, which is sustained by two very thin rulers, and then by another board; when the frame is not big enough. The whole machine thus taken to pieces, will take up no more room than the support itself doth; and so it is very easy to remove from place to place. Now when objects are to be represented in this machine, it must be put together again, as per figure; and the black cloth, for a person to put his head under, hanging upon the sticks, and fastened to the sides of the opening AB, AC, and CD.

47. The use of this second machine is the same as that of the first; but it ought to be observed, that when we incline the machine, the angle of inclination of the mirror and horizon must be made less, by half the inclination of the bottom of the box; and when the machine is somewhat inclined backwards, the said angle must be made greater by a like half. You must likewise observe, that when objects are to be represented for a perpendicular picture, the machine must be placed according to the former part of No. 44. Prints must be fastened to a board entirely separated from the machine, which board must be set upon a support, that may conveniently be moved backwards or forwards, according to necessity.

A Demonstration of the Inclination of the Looking-Glass

48. Let AB be a ray, proceeding from some point of an object. We are to demonstrate, if the line DI hath the inclination given to a picture, and the looking glass GH hath the inclination we have prescribed, that the angle BaF will be equal to the angle BCD. Now to prove this, draw the line FI parallel to the horizon, then the two angles IDF and DFI, of the triangle IDF, are together equal to the angle DIE; but the angle DFI, which is the inclination of the looking glass, is equal to half the angle DIE, less half

the angle IFa; and consequently it is less than the angle FDI, by the quantity of the whole angle IFa. Therefore if the angle IFa be added to the angle DFI, we shall have the angle DFa, equal to the angle FDI: Therefore the angle FaB will be likewise equal to he angle BCD. *Which was to be demonstrated.*

In reasoning nearly after the same manner, we demonstrated what is mentioned concerning the inclination of the mirror, when the box is inclined a little backwards.

Index

Index

inversion: as model for ideology, 1, 2, 5, 6, 9, 12, 13, 26, 40, 42, 49; inversion of the inversion, 2, 6, 50

Kant, Immanuel, 1

labour, 7, 8, 10–12, 14–17
Lecourt, Dominique, 61–62
light chamber [lichtbild], 47–48

Marx, Karl, 1, 3–6, 8, 10–12, 14, 17–19, 21, 26–28, 40, 46, 49, 50; Capital, 6, 7, 12, 13, 16, 19; German Ideology, 1, 6, 12, 13, 19–20; Theses on Feuerbach, 6
metaphor: of the censor or watchman, 22; chemical, 4; Freud's use of, 25, 26; in Marx, 3, 6, 11; in Nietzsche, 29, 30, 39, 40, 42; optical, 6; photographic, 21, 22, 24, 25, 28; of reflection, 3; specular, 3, 4; of sublimation, 4, 5, 11, 13
metaphysics, 3, 6, 9, 26, 28, 40, 41, 44, 45, 46, 50

Nature, 1, 34, 37, 44, 47, 48; in Marx, 10, 16, 32; painting as imitation of, 32, 33, 42
neuroses, 21
Nietzsche, 1, 29, 30, 40, 41, 45, 46, 47, 48, 49

Oedipus, 47
optics, 8, 47, 51, 52; as metaphor, 6, 12, 13, 26

paleonomy, 41
perspective, 14, 31, 32, 35, 39–42, 49, 50–53
perversions, 21
phantasmagoria, 2, 9, 11, 17, 18
photography, 21–26, 28, 30, 49
Plato, 14

reflection, 2–4, 11, 16–17, 32, 36, 37, 48, 52; metaphor of, 3, 61–62; ideas as, 4, 10, 19, 52
religion, 3, 6, 12, 15; religious ideology, 2, 5, 8, 9, 11, 16
repression, 18, 27
retina, 1, 12, 19, 49, 50, 52
Ricardo, 16
Rousseau, Jean-Jacques, 35–40, 48–49

science: history of 3; vision and, 18, 19, 21, 40–42, 49, 50–53; in Marx, 18, 49, 52
screen-memory, 47
specular metaphors, 3–6, 10, 18, 19
Starobinski, Jean, 66
sublimation, see metaphor, of sublimation

transparency, 14, 16, 18, 19, 32–35, 40, 42, 45, 48

unconscious, 13, 14, 22, 23, 26, 30, 41; similarity of functioning to that of camera obscura, 17, 21, 26, 49, 53
use value, 7, 9

watchman, at entrance to consciousness, 22–25, 29